in a
Series?

Happy
Fathers
Day!

J,K&A
+ Stanley

A Sense of Wonder
More moments from an ordinary life

Craig Nagel

authorHOUSE®

AuthorHouse™
1663 Liberty Drive
Bloomington, IN 47403
www.authorhouse.com
Phone: 1-800-839-8640

First published by AuthorHouse   01/16/2012

ISBN: 978-1-4685-4199-1 (sc)
ISBN: 978-1-4685-4198-4 (hc)
ISBN: 978-1-4685-4197-7 (ebk)

Library of Congress Control Number: 2012900505

Printed in the United States of America

Any people depicted in stock imagery provided by Thinkstock are models, and such images are being used for illustrative purposes only.
Certain stock imagery © Thinkstock.

This book is printed on acid-free paper.

Because of the dynamic nature of the Internet, any web addresses or links contained in this book may have changed since publication and may no longer be valid. The views expressed in this work are solely those of the author and do not necessarily reflect the views of the publisher, and the publisher hereby disclaims any responsibility for them.

The cover of this book is a photograph taken by John Hess, Professor of Biology Emeritus, UCM; Brawley Creek Photography (brawleycreek.com) and is used with his permission.

Dedication

To my treasured wife, Claire,
Our beloved son, Christopher,
And the memory of our daughter, Kia.

Also by Craig Nagel

A Place Called Home

Contents

Preface

"In 1972 I was hired to start a weekly newspaper. The owners named it *The Country Echo*. Shortly after getting the paper underway, I bought controlling interest and ran it for the next several years. Later I sold it and turned my hand to other endeavors.

"In 1981 the new owners invited me to start writing a biweekly column for the paper, which I've been doing ever since. I titled it 'The Cracker Barrel,' after the barrel in which crackers were kept in country stores and around which customers lounged for informal conversation. I wanted it to be suggestive of the friendly homespun character of an old-fashioned general store, with nothing too shrill or subversive."

Thus begins the preface to *A Place Called Home*, a book published in 2007 and which, like the present volume, contains essays originally written for "The Cracker Barrel." As with the earlier volume, I've taken the liberty to edit the essays where necessary and to stitch them together with a running narrative in the hope of fitting them into the larger historical context.

Much has changed over the preceding thirty years. It's hard to believe we managed to get along without cell phones or iPods, computers or satellite TV, but we did. As 1981 began, Ronald Reagan was sworn in as president, the Iran hostage crisis came to an end, and the first DeLorean stainless steel car rolled off the production line in Ireland. But life here in the north woods of Minnesota went along as it had for many decades, influenced to large degree by what happened with the weather.

In the preface to *A Place Called Home*, I wrote that one of my greatest satisfactions has come from sharing stories and ideas with readers like you, and concluded with the hope that you might find what follows worthy of your consideration. That hope still stands.

Craig Nagel
Pequot Lakes, Minnesota
Winter 2011-'12

Narrative

In the spring of 1978, six years after starting the Country Echo, I was still working there, managing it for a new owner. But I was itching to start writing novels, and eager to expand and improve our undersized house. In midsummer, I resigned.

My plan was to write every morning and spend the afternoons working on the house, putting up firewood, playing with the kids, and taking time to smell the roses. After several years of sixty- and seventy-hour workweeks, I wanted to redress the balance and spend more time with family and friends. I felt I had a reasonable chance of success, since in years gone by I'd managed to sell some two hundred children's stories and gotten lots of encouragement from various editors. The only hitch might be financial. The money coming in from the sale of our stock in the company was scheduled to be spread over the next five years, but totaled less than a thousand dollars a month. We weren't sure that would be enough to live on, but at least it would be a good start. I set to work writing my first novel, and took to meeting once a week with Jon Hassler, a writer from Brainerd who'd just published his first book, *Staggerford*. Jon was generous with insights and encouragement, and I enjoyed his laconic style of humor.

Like most writers, I'd been keeping a sporadic journal for years, and a look back to it shows that the winter of '78-'79 was a difficult one. On January 11, I noted the temperature at 7 a.m. was 46 below and that the water pipes in the laundry room had frozen up overnight. Three months later, on the 10th of April, an entry states: "It was just announced on the 10 p.m. news that this has been the longest winter in Minnesota since 1888."

That difficult weather pattern continued for the next couple of years. Together with a chronic shortage of money, it made life somewhat trying. I worked every day at revising and polishing my first novel, and finally sent it off, with Jon Hassler's blessing, to his agent in New York. Months passed. As luck would have it, the agent was in Europe on business. When she returned to the States, she was buried with work. In May of 1980, she wrote the following: "You've been extremely patient and I thank you so much. I've read your manuscript a number of times. I am mighty tempted to take it on for representation. You write extremely well and affectingly; and there are some scenes which are really gems. However, after much reflection and given the overload of commitments and backlog, I truly feel I must decline taking on your book."

Sadly, I was unable to place the novel with either an agent or a publisher. After some delay, I started writing another one. I had just finished the first draft, in October of 1981, when the new owners of the Country Echo, Keith and Martha Anderson, suggested I start writing a biweekly column, which I did. I titled it "The Cracker Barrel," as mentioned in the preface, and with Keith and Martha's encouragement, addressed a wide variety of topics, ranging from walks in the woods to the impressions made by an out-of-print book to memories of years gone by.

The one topic I chose to avoid was politics. As Will Rogers observed, "The more you read about politics, the more you got to admit that each party is worse than the other."

Sweet Discontent

We went for a long walk the other day, meandering up through the woods behind our house and then down by the tamarack swamp and along the edge of the marsh, glad to be out of the house, giddy with thoughts of spring. You might say we were taking inventory, though our methods were far from businesslike.

Five minutes into our walk we came upon two depressions in the snow where deer had slept the night before. We crowded around, marveling at the smallness of a curled-up whitetail, fascinated with the discovery of tufts of hair that had frozen into the snowy mattresses. To think that the deer need no houses, no heaters, no blankets nor pillows nor even alarm clocks made us feel vaguely ashamed. Nobody voiced it, but you could feel the shared thought. We two-leggeds are soft and overly complicated.

We walked on.

"Porcupine! Up there in the white pine, on that big branch off to the right."

Again we milled about, all eyes fixed on the bristly brown shape that nestled on the branch like an enormous pine cone. Our excitement slowly ebbed as we realized our prickly brother was fast asleep. Then we saw the places on the trunk of the tree that had been stripped of bark, and we knew that in time the top of the tree would die, and eventually break off in the wind.

We moved on, subdued. And I, for one, began to experience a sense of discontent. I couldn't deny a welling dislike for the porcupine that so wantonly munched on the white pines, dooming them for the sake of breakfast. The further we walked, the more peeled trees we discovered, and the darker my mood became.

It wasn't just the porcupine that prickled my serenity. It was the way everything was dependent on everything else, and the fact (so obvious, and so unpalatable) that man is forever intruding his economic values upon the natural world. What bothered me about the porcupine was that it was destroying valuable trees just for the sake of a meal. And how, pray tell, would I extract their value? By cutting them down, of course, and turning them into lumber.

By the time we reached the tamarack swamp I was near despair. So that's the way it is, I thought. Everything lives at the expense of everything else. At any given moment one is either predator or prey.

Then we came upon the chickadee.

It was perched on a small maple tree growing on a hummock, and the trunk of the tree, no thicker than a baseball bat, was stained dark with liquid.

The chickadee was reaching toward the branch above, from which hung a drop of maple sap. With a deft little thrust of its beak, the chickadee drank from the sweet-water tap, and my bile turned abruptly to nectar.

The law of life is as much giver-and-gift as it is eater-and-eaten.

Fundamentals

The dark blue spine of the book bore a single word: *Masonry*. It stood straight among its leaning companions, as if built on a firmer foundation than theirs. I took it from the shelf and read the subtitle: "A Handbook of Tools, Materials, Methods, and Directions." By Kenneth Holmes Bailey. Copyright 1945.

The antique shop in which I stood faded from mind as I leafed through the book. Chapter 1—Concrete. Chapter 2—Plastering. Chapter 3—Stucco. Subsequent chapters dealt with brickwork, concrete, glass block, etc. I turned to the introduction and commenced to read. The writing style was brisk, no-nonsense. I finished the introduction and paged onward, stopping now and then to read a sentence or two, study an illustration, examine a table of weights or dimensions.

Little by little the tone of the book became evident. "It is the responsibility of the workman to keep his tools in satisfactory condition." "Quick setting of plaster may be caused by a number of conditions, but carelessness in selecting or mixing the ingredients on the job is the chief cause." "When stuccoing, the work should proceed ahead of the sun, i.e., beginning with the south wall in the early morning and working around to the west, north and east sides as rapidly as possible. This system allows the successive coats of stucco sufficient time to get their initial set before the sun speeds up the drying action."

I bought the book, took it home, read it. From beginning to end, the message was unvarying. A proper job requires proper tools. Materials must be carefully selected and correctly installed. Cleanliness, planning, and unswerving attention to detail are necessary to insure successful completion of the task at hand. The workman who does shoddy work cheats his employer, the client, and himself. Good work depends more than anything else on a firm grasp of fundamentals.

When I finished reading the book, I set it aside and pondered. It is unlikely that such a book would find a publisher today. The tone would be deemed overly moralistic, for one thing. The title would have to be changed to something catchier—*Finding Your Bliss Through Brickwork*, or *How to Profit From the Housing Industry Collapse*, or maybe *The Sensuous Stonemason*. The photos and illustrations, though clear and to the point, would have to be changed from black and white to retina-teasing color, which in turn would mean the price of the book would have to be raised from its original $1.60 to $45.00 or so.

But no. A book like this would never make the best-seller list, not even with lots of photos of sexy women laborers mixing mortar or prancing on the scaffold showing off designer jeans. And if it didn't hit best-seller status, how could you expect to sell movie rights or spin-offs such as T-shirts, posters, or CD's?

Forget it, friends. This book will never do. This is a book about fundamentals.

A Green Bough

More years ago than I care to admit, I was a fuzzy-faced freshman in college with large dreams of changing the world.

I was glad, finally, to be on my own, away from the watchful eyes of my parents, away from the busybody neighbors and the woefully backward small town in which I'd spent my childhood. When I came back at Thanksgiving, the sense of having outgrown my origins was even more acute.

Everybody seemed so small! My parents, my brothers and sisters, old buddies from high school who hadn't gone on to college; they all suffered from some mysterious dwarfism. Their concerns, so real to me a few months earlier, now smacked of the commonplace, the trivial, the truly boring. Compared to the larger issues which occupied my collegiate mind, their interest in everyday things like the price of gasoline or how the local basketball team was faring seemed pitifully unimportant.

I remember yawning a lot that first holiday home from school. Yawning and going for long solitary walks. It's bad enough to feel like an outsider; it's considerably worse to feel that way when you're *home*. So I walked, and asked myself a hundred questions. Didn't they care about developing the mind? Hadn't they heard about the atomic bomb? Were they all so obtuse as to not understand that Socrates himself had said the unexamined life was not worth living?

Time passed. My initial hopes of infusing the world with dazzling new insight began to shrink. Toward the end of my college years, I became preoccupied with merely trying to figure out what I could do to assemble a major and graduate. By that time even going to college seemed trivial and void of value. Then, in my senior year, I stumbled into the study of things Oriental.

Even now, across decades of memories, those months of reading and reflection seem fresh and green and wonderful, an oasis of the spirit. For it was then that my mental fevers began to subside, and I commenced to understand that all things are related to one another, and that the mind, if not kept in harmony and balance with the hands and heart, can turn into something tumorous and sick.

I remember in particular the day I came across a fragment of a Chinese poem. I happened to be sitting outside, under a newly budded maple tree. The air was alive with the humming of bees and the flutter of dozens of little blue butterflies. The book fell open as if by magic, and before me on the page were these few words: "Keep a green bough in your heart, and a singing bird will come."

Ever since, I've been trying to do as the poet suggested. On occasion, I've forgotten—sometimes for months. But I've noticed that when I remember, good things happen, and I don't think that's just coincidence.

When you allow your mind to turn in on itself, consumed by your private worries, the world has a way of growing bleak and cheerless. As a young student, I managed to cut myself off from the people and things around me, erecting a wall of sophomoric self-importance through which nothing good could pass. No wonder everything seemed pointless and boring and dull: all I was seeing was myself!

The truth is that the world is filled to overflowing with adventures, thousands of which await our permission to occur. All we need to do is open ourselves to them. If we keep ourselves green and lively, they will surely come.

Ed's Dad

My first boss was a man named Ed. At the time I started work, Ed was right around 40, with a young son, Eddie, and a father nearing retirement.

I don't recall Ed's father's name, but I do recall what happened to him. I remember coming to work on a Monday morning and learning that Ed's dad was getting excited at the prospect of pulling the plug. He'd worked at the same plant in Chicago for nearly half a century, walking to work in the morning and walking home at night. Rain or shine, winter and summer, year after year after year, his routine was the same.

Now it was time to quit.

"Mom talked him into buying new clothes for the retirement party," said Ed. "New shoes, new suit, new tie. He hates to spend money on himself, but this way he'll have a decent outfit to wear at weddings and funerals after he's retired, which makes sense, since he'll probably live another 20 years. He's healthy as an ox."

Finally the big day came. Ed's dad put on his new duds, kissed his wife goodbye, and walked for one final time to the place where he'd spent so much of his life. By all accounts he enjoyed the retirement party. Cake, coffee, and lots of good-natured ribbing. At the end his boss gave him a gold-plated watch and his coworkers presented him with a new fishing rod, since they knew he loved to fish and intended to spend a chunk of his leisure time on the water. He thanked them, wiped back a tear or two, shook hands all around, and started home, no doubt humming to himself as he imagined what life would be like without having to return to work.

When he got home, he showed his wife the gifts he'd been given and told her everything had gone well, except that on the way home his right foot had begun to hurt.

"New shoes too tight?" she asked.

"No. It's in the heel."

He took off his shoes and discovered the problem. A nail from the heel had worked its way up through the inner sole and poked through his sock into his skin.

The next morning his heel was red and throbbing. He soaked it in warm water and considered going to the doctor, but decided to wait until after the weekend.

By Monday his ankle and calf were mottled with red streaks. His wife insisted he call the family doc, which he did. Later that day he was diagnosed with blood poisoning and taken to the hospital. But it was already too late. A few days later he was dead.

The undertakers laid Ed's dad out in his new suit. According to Ed, several of the mourners commented on how nice he looked.

A few weeks after the funeral, Ed's mom gave the watch to Ed and the fishing rod to Eddie.

She said Ed's dad would have wanted it that way.

Sand Roads

For nearly half a century we've lived at the end of a sand road. Not the same road, but a sand road—and all sand roads have much in common.

We've sometimes hated it in the spring. That week or two or three between when the snow melts and the frost goes out, that's the worst time. Puddles grow into ponds. Ruts become canyons. All vehicles take on the same sandy hue. Back when our kids were still in school, the Spirit-in-charge-of-watching-over-roads would hear two sets of contradictory requests: the youngsters hoping the school bus would get stuck, and my wife praying it would not.

Each year, by the time the frost is gone, we've made plans to haul in more fill. Some nice Class 5. Many yards of nice Class 5. Hang the expense—we'll fight those ruts no longer. Someday maybe we'll even have it blacktopped. Yes, by tar—a road so smooth and firm and water-shedding as to make the pickup ride like a Rolls Royce.

Then the hieroglyphics start appearing.

Fresh grouse tracks by the power line cut. The straight dot-to-dot of fox prints. The meandering lines left by a doe and two yearlings. Hoof prints from a neighbor's horse.

And on it goes through spring and summer into fall. Each day's walk reveals new scribbles in the sand; mute messages from birds and snakes and furbearers (ranging in size from shrew to raccoon to coyote to black bear), delicate notations from insects, the scribed arcs of wind-swung plants, even the skid marks of fallen leaves.

A momentary shower leaves its dotted inscription pockmarked over the squiggles left by a turtle's tail.

We watch, enthralled, as birds take dust baths in the old sand road.

We note where larger birds seek gizzard grit.

We stop to study the mysterious industry of ants, and let our eyes wander along the twisty lines of beetle tracks.

And when it rains enough to wash the dust away, we find the road transformed into a treasure chest, speckled with shiny agates aglow like drops of fallen sunset.

It's then that we have a change of heart, and find ourselves forsaking the earlier resolutions of spring. Now the true value of our sand road stands revealed.

Will we pave such a precious place of riches? Not on your life! What's convenience compared to this living notebook, this half-mile-long recorder of natural drama?

No thanks, Mr. Progress. We'll keep to the old ways, washboard and all.

Papa's Magnificent Motorcar

O ver the weekend I had several long talks with an old friend, during which a number of half-forgotten memories surfaced, including thoughts of a rather remarkable automobile I had the good fortune of getting to know back in the 1960's.

At the time I was a young GI stationed in Germany. I lived off-post in the village of Eschenbach, east of Stuttgart, in the top floor of a house owned by Mr. and Mrs. Albert Wucherer, more commonly known as Papa and Mama.

Papa, a master machinist in his early 50's, was by nature and necessity a man of thrifty habits, careful to purchase things that gave him full value for his money. As a young man following World War II, he had filled his transportation needs with a motorcycle, adding a sidecar after his marriage to Mama. The sidecar worked OK even after their first child was born, but with the coming of a second, they'd been forced to get something bigger, which brings us to his automobile.

He owned a vintage Peugeot, bought new many years earlier. The car was black and basic, but comfortable to drive and modest in its fuel-eating habits. Henry Ford Sr. would have thought it superb.

Why? Because everything about it came apart, permitting its owner full control over his automotive destiny.

The fenders came off in minutes, attached by a mere handful of bolts. The running boards, the hood and trunk, the bumpers, the doors, the grill—all could be removed with the twist of a wrench.

It was my good fortune to help Papa with the fourth rebuilding of his automobile. Every four or five years he followed the same procedure, completely dismantling the machine into its original components.

We took the body apart and hammered out the dings, sanded off the old paint, and applied six coats of black lacquer, hand-rubbed between coats. We took the chrome parts off, put them in the back seat of my VW bug, and took them to be rechromed. We removed the seats and took them to the upholstery shop, ripped out the carpeting to use as a pattern for its replacement, installed fresh tires on the newly painted wheels.

The engine was a study in simplicity, yielding up its parts with a minimum of fuss. The cylinders had sleeves which Papa removed and replaced with new ones. The pistons and shafts and valves and rockers all went with him to work, perched in the basket of his bicycle. During lunch break he honed and turned and polished them as he saw fit, and when he brought them back home and put them in the engine, everything was factory fresh.

Finally the day came when we reinstalled the engine, bolted on the last of the sparkling chrome, dusted off the new black carpeting, and climbed in for a test run.

The little car ran like a Swiss watch.

Papa was pleased. "Ja," he said, grinning at Mama. "It's nice to be rich, eh? Every few years and poof! Another brand-new car."

That was long ago and I've since lost touch with Mama and Papa. Chances are they've passed on. But I wouldn't be surprised if they drove their little car for the balance of their driving lives, taking delight in every mechanical rebirth, quietly wondering to themselves why friends and neighbors complained of how hard it was to make ends meet.

Narrative

Later in the fall of 1981, with the cupboards bare, it became clear that we needed more money. After some discussion with my brother, Bill, we decided to resume building fireplaces, which we'd done together every summer before I quit to start the newspaper. It was still my hope to sell one or both of the novels and become a full-time writer. Unfortunately, the manuscripts kept coming back to me unsold. One was even returned on Christmas Eve, which did little to raise my Yuletide spirits. But if life had taught me anything to this point, it was that you had to persevere, and so I kept resubmitting the manuscripts, hoping for the best.

The winter of '81-'82 was another harsh one, which made doing masonry work all but impossible. According to a journal entry dated January 11, "Yesterday, according to NBC, was the coldest day in the United States in the 20th century. 26 below in Chicago, with wind chills here in Minnesota down to -100." But cold or not, I had a family to feed and ongoing bills to pay. Toward the end of January my lifelong friend Bill Walker and I trailered his Belgian workhorse, Maude, from Park Rapids to our homestead outside of Pequot Lakes and, on a nearby permit from the Potlatch Paper Company, commenced cutting and selling firewood. A journal entry from the 5th of February states:

"Last night mercury nudged -40, and high today will probably be -10. Air in the morning is viscous with frost crystals, giving it a pearly sheen. After sun comes up, air sparkles."

Working with Maude proved delightful. She quickly learned how to skid the fallen tree trunks to the landing once we'd hooked the skid chain to her harness, and the clink and creak of the harness and the huff of her breath made a pleasant punctuation to the snarl of our chainsaws. The only trouble we had was when a log she was skidding got jammed against a stump, whereupon Maude, as she had been trained to do, would rear up, preparing to lunge forward, and Bill and I would start screaming for her to stop, knowing the old leather harness and tug lines would never withstand the strain of her 1800 pounds. Luckily we had a neighbor, Chuck Knierim, with an industrial-grade sewing machine and a rivet gun. By the end of winter the harness had put on significant weight, in the form of leather patches and dozens and dozens of rivets.

Given the difficult conditions of a harder-than-average winter, I doubt our logging venture actually proved all that profitable. But it did allow us to experience working in the woods, and gave us a sense of deep respect for those who harvest trees for a living. And I can report with certainty that sandwiches and coffee never taste better than when devoured by a hungry lumberjack.

When, in the spring, we moved Maude back to Park Rapids, our homestead was the poorer for her absence. As I wrote in the journal, "There is something about having a large creature around that calms the spirit. Each morning, when we went out to bring her water and feed, she would whinny in anticipation. On warm days she would roll on the ground and prance up and down in her little corral. Her huge brown eyes seemed to see everything, and to accept the world as it is."

Winter Guests

I t happened on an autumn Saturday many years ago.

In the house we lived in then, I'd built a little desk with a bank of drawers in an alcove off the dining room. We used it for paying bills and writing letters. Over time the drawers had filled with canceled checks and various receipts and tax returns. On that fateful morning, as I sat eating breakfast, I heard a rustle of paper from one of the drawers.

I knew in an instant the sound meant mice. Every fall the woodland critters decided to spend the coming winter inside our house. You couldn't blame them, really; 70 above beats 30 below for anything but an ice cube.

But you couldn't exactly welcome them, either. They chewed things to pieces and ravaged your pantry and left unsightly little souvenirs on the kitchen counter. Once we'd returned from a two-week absence and found an entire dresser drawer filled with nuggets of dog food, patiently hauled upstairs from the kitchen to the bedroom. Our general rule was *Live and Let Live*—but with mice we amended the rule to read *We'll Live Inside and We'll Let You Live Outside.*

By the time I finished breakfast the rustling had stopped. I took the dishes to the sink, slurped a final shot of coffee, and walked to the desk to investigate.

The top drawer was clean, as was the middle one. But when I opened the bottom drawer, I saw that the contents were seriously trashed. The top several papers had been gnawed into confetti, and the papers below them were peppered with mouse poop. In the angle formed by the front and one side of the drawer lay a crude nest built of paper scraps, lint, and hair. The nest was as big as my hand and contained one adult female mouse, sprawled on her side.

How did I know she was female and adult? Because of the babies she was nursing.

The babies were hairless and pink, no bigger than the last joint of your little finger. They lay bunched together in a compact row, their tiny mouths clamped to mama's teats, busily sucking milk, their sightless eyes still covered by protective membrane. In memory I count five of them.

A sterner-hearted person might have dispatched them on the spot. I, instead, felt a wave of pity. Mama mouse had done a lot of work preparing a nursery for the little ones. It didn't seem right to kill them. I found an empty shoebox, lifted the nest and its occupants into the box, and carried it outside, where I placed it on the ground some fifty feet from the house. Worried that our dogs might mistake the little family for a morning snack, I found another, larger, box, cut a tiny door in one end, and placed it over the first. As an added precaution I weighted the outer box down with a sizeable stone and went back into the house to wash my hands.

The day passed uneventfully, filled with prewinter chores. The dogs didn't bother the displaced mice and by nightfall I figured the little family had taken the hint and moved into a nice warm pile of fallen leaves.

Then, after supper, I heard a squeak come from one of the drawers. When I opened it I could hardly believe my eyes. There, ensconced in a brand-new nest, lay Mama and her suckling brood.

"How is this possible?" I asked my wife. "She must have worked her tail off."

"No, it's still there."

"You know what I mean. Think of the effort involved, finding her way back into the house, building a whole new nest and then hauling each of the babies back from out in the yard and . . . Jeez." I lapsed into silence, overwhelmed and amazed.

"So what do you want to do?" she asked.

"I don't think we have a choice."

"Me neither." She pushed the drawer shut. "Later, maybe, if it gets too bad, we'll put out traps. But right now I think they should stay."

The Day the Old Barn Fell

It happened on Wednesday, February 3, 1982.

Sometime that afternoon the old barn collapsed beneath a winter's weight of snow and settled back to the earth from which, years ago, it had sprung. It went to its fate without fanfare or complaint. No theatrics, no ear-splitting crash or boom. Nothing like that. It just quietly sprawled in the snow.

A friend called that evening to relay the news. "A sad thing happened today," she said. "You know the barn on East Clark Lake Road, the one Col. Thorp built? Well, today the old barn fell."

She went on to explain that the barn, built in 1905, was the last building Thorp had built. Over the years, the colonel's barn had become something of a local landmark. Referred to simply as "the barn on East Clark Lake Road," it was known and loved by locals and tourists alike. Many a visitor stopped to photograph the weatherworn old building. Now 77 years old, it had given up its long struggle against wind and gravity and settled quietly into the snow.

With it goes a testimonial to an uncommonly lived life. Freeman Thorp was not an ordinary man. As an artist, Thorp was feted for his portraits of American presidents, starting with Lincoln and continuing through Grant, Garfield, McKinley and Cleveland; to him goes the honor of having painted more presidential portraits than any other artist. A native of Ohio, Thorp came to Minnesota in middle age, hoping the climate here would benefit his son, Clark, who was dying of tuberculosis. The colonel was down on his luck when he arrived, having suffered acute financial reverses in an ill-fated investment venture. Shortly after arriving, son Clark (after whom Clark Lake is named) died.

Lesser men might have given up. Freeman Thorp dug in. On the shores of Clark Lake he built a terraced orchard and garden and began exporting produce. To finance the building of a palatial new home, he took up his paintbrush and did portraits of dozens of famous Minnesotans: business tycoons, political figures, lumber kings, etc. He made his life, like his land, yield abundant fruit. And finally, in 1905, he built a big barn.

No doubt other barns have fallen to earth this winter. With each of them goes a story, a tiny patch of history on the quilt of our common heritage.

We are saddened by their passing. Their familiarity comforts us. They link us with the past. The texture and line of weathered pine and canted wall provide a visual haven for the eye grown weary of the ugliness of modern slapdash structures. When they disappear, the landscape feels diminished.

On a deeper plane, what we mourn is the passing of life. We want our old barns to stay put, to stand forever. But of course they don't. Change, not permanence, is the central law of life. And though we mourn, life must—and will—go on.

The Joys of Journaling

1 984, aside from its infamy as the title of George Orwell's bleak book, is a year of note for me.

This is the year my journal comes of age. On January 6, to be exact. It was on that day in 1963 that I began to keep a journal.

Now keeping a journal is not the mainstream sort of hobby it was back in the Victorian era. But the rules are pretty much the same. Step one is to decide what sort of journal you might want to keep.

A journal (from the Latin word *diurnalis*, "of the day") is in essence a daybook. Bookkeepers keep journals as books of original entry. Legislatures and other such bodies keep journals as records of transactions. The word is also used to denote newspapers and magazines dealing with matters of current interest.

In its most common form, a journal is used as a diary.

Mine isn't.

Mine is—let's be honest—sporadic. Looking back, I find whole years and sizeable portions thereof that passed unnoticed in my fitful record.

Summers are most at risk. In summer a person tends to be busy outdoors. So what happens is that the events, ideas, anecdotes, and personalities of the colder months get an unfair share of coverage in my journal. Too bad, but that's the way it is.

What do I record?

All sorts of things.

The temperature, if it's outrageous or soothing enough.

My weight, if it starts creeping up.

Observations, mainly. Ideas, scenes, quotations, little insights into the nature of things. Many of my journal entries are about nature itself: the date the juncos returned; when the first raspberries ripened; a glowing description of the northern lights.

Some entries (usually hard to read afterward) are made in the middle of the night after waking with what seems an awesomely profound idea. Others are as prosaic as lunchtime, noted in careful penmanship, sometimes bejeweled with figures and glyphs.

Here and there one finds a poem or a fragment thereof, stitched to the paper with ink to keep it from escaping. Or a quick how-to-build-it sketch of something I'll get around to making one of these days.

A journal—at least *my* journal—is an inward thing, a semisecret place. Reading through the many volumes of it that have come to populate the shelf through 21 years, I find much that now seems embarrassing, sophomoric. But even that gives value to the journal, for in it you see a record of your growth.

If you've never kept a journal, now is a good time to start. The new year offers a perfect chance to list your goals, to note your resolutions, to confide your private observations of the celebrations just past.

A journal is a friend. It listens patiently to all you have to say. It is offended by nothing. And best of all, it never talks back.

Spring Thoughts

In most other parts of the country, spring eases its way into your life.

First the snow begins to melt. Later puddles gather and sit around for several weeks, soaking up the sunshine. Temperatures rise gradually.

From start to finish, the process of converting from winter to summer takes a couple of months. Spring is a bona fide *season*.

Not so in northern Minnesota.

Here we go from winter to summer faster than you can say, "Tourist!" One day you're so sick of snowbanks you're thinking of paddling to Hawaii in your duck boat, and the next day you keel over from heat exhaustion because you forgot to take your long johns off. Things move rapidly here. If you oversleep on the wrong day of the year, you may wake up to find that, while you were having erotic dreams about life in the tropics, spring has come and gone.

Considering the length of our winters, perhaps spring is something we can't really afford much of, for fear of cutting into our all-too-limited summertime. Still, it seems almost brutal to slam shift from the deep freeze to the oven without a decent interlude of thawing.

But Mother Nature doesn't seem to mind.

Migrating birds return, frogs work their way up out of the mud, crocuses burst into bloom, and the buds on the popple trees swell up like popcorn, all with nary a fuss.

Saturday we woke to find our birdfeeder jammed with half a dozen red squirrels and a dozen hungry chickadees, and the ground below quivering with hordes of returning juncos. Later we watched a shrike spear a junco and eat it for lunch. And at dusk we heard the *peent* of a woodcock as he began to stake out this year's territory.

On Sunday the sky was alive with the honking of returning geese, while down by the shop newly energized chipmunks played hide-and-seek in a rock pile.

All of this occurred in the immediate aftermath of a blizzard, with the ground buried under many inches of snow.

What causes such profusion, such breaking-forth of life?

There are many scientific reasons, such as photo-periodism (the lengthening daylight), the rise in ambient temperature, the movement of species into areas where food (buds and insects) becomes available, and so on.

But you wonder, too, if there isn't some sort of inward urge to simply be done with winter, some ancient yearning to put snowbanks and lethargy aside.

Maybe spring comes in part because all creatures *will* it to come.

Or maybe it's just because it's time to start the baseball season.

In Praise of Fiction

A long time ago, when I was a junior in high school, I recall having a minor argument with a good friend over the merit of fiction versus nonfiction. Pete loved to read novels, especially science fiction. I, on the other hand, could see little sense in wasting time on stuff that wasn't real.

"But it's just as real as that hot rod magazine you're reading," argued Pete. "More real, in a way. These stories make you think, man. They stretch your imagination."

"Yeah? So what? What good does it do to sit there pretending you're in some dream world? No thanks. Give me something practical. Something helpful. Something down to earth."

Now, decades later, I'm embarrassed every time I remember our conversation. How could I have been so unaware? More importantly, how could I have denied myself access to one of the most exciting aspects of being alive?

Fiction, I now know, has a power and a penetration that mere reality can never attain. Fiction allows us to delve into parts of the world otherwise unknowable. It endows us with magical capabilities the workaday world denies or ignores.

Jonis Agee put it this way: "Writing is a way to enter people's lives and imaginations. What fiction does is allow you to see the way other people live, or how they image themselves living."

In this sense, fiction acts like an x-ray, permitting us to see things that are otherwise hidden from view. The more we see, the better we understand things. And the better we understand, the larger and wiser we become. Having once read, for instance, a novel such as Richard Wright's *Black Boy*, we can never again relapse into a complacent racism, for we have experienced through the power of fiction what it really feels like to be black and poor and scorned by nearly everyone, and through this experience our deepest parts are changed.

Fiction can amuse and annoy and excite and depress, but it almost always makes us grow. In book after book after book, it presents us with the possibilities of our shared humanity. In this way it reveals truth that everyday reality often obscures. At its best, it can inspire us to surmount our humdrum habits and aspire to moments of excellence.

Man is the species that becomes. We transcend our yesterdays with dreams and visions of our tomorrows. My friend Pete was right. Visions don't come from reality, from things as they are. Visions come from our capacity to imagine.

On Cultivation

F or the past several years it's been fashionable to rhapsodize about all things natural. Our breakfast cereals, our skin lotions, our methods of delivering babies and decorating our homes—all have "gone natural."

Along the way, some sacred cows have taken ill.

We have discovered, for example, that many of the artificial foods and medicinal aids touted on TV have little nutritional or medical value, and that some of them are quite unhealthy.

We've begun to understand that prevention, rather than medication, is the most effective way to ward off disease, and that what we eat affects how healthy we are.

A growing number of us have turned away from the overprocessed concoctions of the recent past and taken to our collective bosom that which is less adorned and not so laced with mysterious preservatives.

But as any gardener will tell you, the natural way has limitations, for the plain fact is that nature is innately rampant and indifferent to the wants of man.

The trick, somehow, is to learn to work with nature while keeping our own ends in mind. Building up the soil, for instance, is a more effective route toward consistently good crops than is spraying the soil with herb- and pesticides. Healthy soil produces healthy foods, which in turn produce healthy people.

But even when we learn to cooperate with the natural processes, we still have to work if we want rewards. As disgruntling as the fact may be, there are no real shortcuts to anything worthwhile—and it is here that the recent emphasis on all things natural may be dangerously misleading.

To grow good vegetables or a durable set of values, cultivation is necessary. You can't just plant your seeds or give birth to your children and leave the rest up to Mother Nature—not if you want results that bring you pride and satisfaction.

Life, it turns out, is quite a row to hoe, and hoe we must. The weeds spring up without respite, whether in the garden or in one's larger life. Unless we are willing to let our best qualities be choked out, we must cultivate them with care, determination, and unending diligence.

Narrative

As the months passed by and more and more of my essays appeared in the Echo, I began to get feedback from readers. Most of the letters and comments I received were positive, though a handful weren't. Many folks were simply curious. Over the years, the most frequently asked query from readers is the one about origin: "Where do you get your ideas?"

As any truthful writer will admit, this is an interesting question, and one which doesn't admit of a single, simple answer. In fact the ideas come from all over the place, and sometimes take their sweet time arriving. Some come from basic observation: you see something that tickles your fancy, and scribble down notes. Young grouse feeding in the dew-laden grass; the sudden profusion of new leaves in the spring; the profound joy you feel during a family reunion. Other things you see might affect you adversely, and raise your ire to a fine righteous heat. An ongoing dispute with the bears, say, or the sudden regret you feel after dropping a large red oak for firewood.

Mister Independent

In common with many Americans, I fancy myself an independent. Not so much politically, but in a deeper, more thoroughgoing way.

Others may need the comfort of belonging to this group or that. Others less feisty may crave the constant approval of their peers. But true independents like us think for ourselves, make our own way in this world, and don't rely on the government to do our work for us.

Take, for instance, last Friday.

Wakened from my slumbers by the waspy buzz of the alarm clock, I rubbed the sleep from my eyes, plodded to the bathroom, started the coffee brewing, pulled on my jeans and work boots, peered out the window at the pink-streaked sky, and smiled. "Life is good," I murmured, aware that the weekend was one day away. "Very good indeed."

A few minutes later, sitting out in the screen porch sipping coffee and listening to the arias of orioles and the cackle of nesting geese, a dissonant thought assailed me.

"Alarm clock," I muttered, and wondered who made it. Without it, I'd still be asleep. I tried to push the thought aside. Instead it branched into a half-dozen new topics: the bathroom, the coffeepot, the coffee itself, the jeans, the boots, the window. Where did all these things come from?

In the case of the bathroom, I'd done much of my own plumbing, cut and soldered the copper pipes myself. But others had made them, and before that others had mined and smelted the copper, and even before that others had made the equipment that made mining and smelting possible.

Same with the coffeepot.

And someone in warmer climes had grown and harvested the coffee I now drank, and elsewhere others had grown the cotton and woven the denim and sewed the jeans I wore, and others had raised the cattle and tanned the hides and crafted the boots in which I walked.

As for the window through which I'd stared at the sky, that, too, was the work of others. Loggers, sash builders, glassmakers, truckers—all had a hand in producing the window I had placed in the wall.

"But," said the voice of independence, "you *bought* all this stuff. If you hadn't gone out and worked your tail off, the stuff' would still be sitting in a store somewhere."

I felt a little surge of returning pride. What the heck. The voice was right. It was still up to independent people like myself to make things happen. I swallowed the last of the coffee, grabbed the lunch my wife had made, and strode out to my truck, ready to conquer the world.

Sure, I thought, as I backed out of the garage, we all lean on each other a little. True, I can't make a truck by myself, or the tools it contains, or the gas it runs on. But that doesn't mean I'm *dependent*.

I drove out the driveway to the paved township road, then turned right onto the paved county road, and right again onto the paved state highway. Annoying thoughts about the construction and maintenance of roads nibbled at my brain.

Enough! I cranked the radio up loud and beat time to the music on the steering wheel. There. Much better. Drown out those niggling doubts and questions. Take pride in who you are.

Mister Independent.

Emergent Miracles

I stare out the window of my writing studio, surrounded by trees, and my eyes slowly focus on the leaves. Oak leaves, birch leaves, popple leaves, the tubular needles of red pines and white pines and spruce. All the leaves. Good Lord, there are multiple thousands of them, millions perhaps, just in the viewing space framed by my window.

Each of the deciduous leaves is a recent arrival, not long emerged from its hiding place inside a bud. A month ago, staring out the same window, I would have seen only a skeletal framework of branches and twigs among the pines. Were I possessed of x-ray vision, I might have seen deeper, and glimpsed the stirring of sap inside the bones of the leafless forest. Instead I saw only bark.

So much lies hidden from view. I see the trunk and branches of a tree and think I am seeing the whole tree, but in fact I'm seeing only a part. Beneath the ground an entire root system lies buried, fated never to be sensed by anyone but voles and gophers and earthworms. The realization prompts a pang of humility: next time I think I am seeing the whole of another person, I'll try to remind myself of this. Below the surface of a fellow human much lies buried and unseeable, just like the roots of a tree.

My gaze returns to the leaves. A puff of breeze makes them twist and skitter, as if dancing to unheard tunes. Tethered by their stems to the twigs from which they've sprung, their range of movement is much less than ours, their position in the universe fixed to a space of mere inches. But within that small space, miracles occur.

From the first light of dawn to the end of the day, each leaf is busy making food. Unlike their counterparts in the animal kingdom, who essentially cannibalize other life forms, plants make food, and they do it as if by magic. Using only sunlight, carbon dioxide, and water, they manage to create organic compounds, the bread of life. According to my trusty *Encyclopedia Britannica*, the rate at which members of the animal kingdom die and consume each other is so high that they would all disappear from the earth within the lifetime of a human generation were it not for plants providing this recombination of organic matter.

As if this weren't enough, in the process of photosynthesis each leaf imparts a small amount of oxygen into the air, which goes to form the breath of life. Without the relentless work of leaves, the rest of us would have nothing to eat or breathe.

Nor do their gifts stop here. In the act of making food and oxygen, leaves pump water into the air, drawn up from the roots of the tree and expelled from the underside of each leaf. It is estimated that a mature oak gives off several hundred gallons of water a day during the growing season; water which, in the oak tree's absence, would remain locked in the soil.

I close my eyes to give my mind a rest. The debt of gratitude we owe the leaves is staggering. Without them, we could not exist.

Tools

One of the hallmarks of being human is the use of tools. Unlike other animals, we need tools. Our survival as well as much of our satisfaction derives from our ability to conceive and produce and utilize objects not readily found in nature. From the first chipped stones on through the microprocessors in our computers, human history is essentially the story of tool use.

In its most limited sense, a tool is defined as an instrument used or worked by hand, such as a hammer or a spear, devised to allow us to exert greater force than our bare fingers or palms or fists are capable of doing. Tigers and bears come equipped with claws; man relies upon some form of cutting blade. An elephant can wrap its trunk around a log and move it; we make use of rollers or levers, or, by extension, a hoist.

When you boil it all down, most tools help us perform one of four functions or combinations thereof—cutting, moving, measuring, or fastening. In this way, tools allow us to transform things from their original state into something new: to alter their contours, as when we chop or saw a tree into boards or pulpwood; combine two or more separate things together, as when we join joists and studs and rafters to build a house; or transform a thing into something radically different, as when we shred and stew pulpwood into paper, or melt sand into glass.

As might be expected, the tools we use affect us. Swinging a hammer year after year is apt to cause bursitis. Clacking away at a keyboard can trigger carpal tunnel syndrome. Operating heavy equipment may reduce our range of hearing. But there is a brighter side to this. Prolonged and competent use of these same tools, or any others, can bring us pleasure and pride as our ability to use them approaches artistry. Whether saw or shovel, scalpel or spatula, sewing machine or spinnaker, the deft use of tools delights us in unique and lasting ways.

Good tools, well-designed and properly constructed, are a joy to work with. Shoddy tools are a different story. There are few things in life more vexing than to work with poorly made tools. Your hand recoils from their unwelcoming handle. Your back twists from their unbalanced weight. They transform your fingers into thumbs, your smile into a scowl. Prolonged exposure to bad tools can cause serious and deep-seated feelings of discontent. We might think it's the job we dislike, when in fact it may be the tools we use to do the job.

A fascinating study could be made of the cultural differences among tools. The European hand saw, for example, cuts only on the down stroke, while the Japanese saw cuts on the up stroke. In our culture, force is poured out; in theirs it's pulled in.

From the birthing room to the funeral parlor, our lives are shaped by the tools we use and the thousands of objects we make with them. Take away our tools and we would perish. In a profound and ongoing way, tools are what make us human.

Eleven Reasons

For the past several days, I've been privileged to spend the first half-hour of the morning watching a family of grouse. To do this requires a very small outlay of energy on my part. In fact, all it entails is filling my coffee cup and walking out into the screen porch.

Once seated, I sit and sip and wait for the grouse to announce themselves, which they do via a gentle cooing cluck, something that sounds like a cross between a mourning dove and a barnyard hen.

Most mornings I hear them long before I see them, no doubt in part because the lawn near the porch is rather shaggy. But soon the first mottled brown body comes poking out among the clumps of overgrown grass, and then another and another and another. Heads down, pecking steadily at bits of greenery and an occasional bug, they work their way toward the porch, apparently unconcerned that they're nearing a human zone.

As near as I can tell there are eleven in the family: two adult birds which I take to be Mama and Papa, and nine youngsters in various stages of development. Several have not yet grown tail feathers, and have curving hindquarters that end in a near-perfect point. All of the younger grouse look slightly unkempt, as if they have not yet heard about preening. Two or three of them sport little tufts of feathers atop their heads, giving them a particularly jaunty look.

As they approach the edge of the porch, I slowly lean forward in my chair, until my face is less than a yard away from the little band of foragers below me. Up close, the intricate patterns of their feathers are overpoweringly beautiful. I try to imagine how a human might go about trying to design something so complex and effective using only browns and grays and whites, but my brain whimpers at the thought.

Two stubby-tailed youngsters suddenly freeze in position. Trouble is afoot. A moment later our cat, Skeeter, makes a dramatic pounce into the tangled grass. In an instant the air is full of grouse, at least two of which are larger than the cat. Skeeter, the intrepid hunter, turns and runs for her life. She's not used to flushing eleven of anything.

Minutes pass and one by one the mottled young sail down from the ironwood branches into which they have taken refuge and resume pecking in the grass. One enterprising fellow discovers the greenish-white berries hanging from a small dogwood tree. He stands on tiptoe, craning his head up as high as he can, but the berries remain tantalizingly out of reach. Abruptly he hunkers down and then springs upward, snatching a berry at the top of his jump. The technique is soon imitated by one of the others, and for a final few minutes I sit grinning at the outrageous sight of half-grown grouse leaping up and down gathering breakfast.

I finish the last of the coffee, watch as one final berry is plucked, then turn to the tasks of the day. Later, driving to work, the thought occurs that I now have eleven more reasons for being glad to be alive.

The Reunion

We'd been talking about it for weeks, going over the details of who would sleep where, who would be arriving when, where we'd be able to find room for everybody to eat in case of rain. It would be a family reunion, the first in several years, to be held here in the woods at our place.

The last few days of preparation grew fatiguing. Too much left to do, not enough time to do it in. But everybody pitched in, and the last of the weeds fell to the weed eater, the windows of the house were washed, and the mess in the shop somehow dissolved, leaving us with a large area to serve as dining hall.

On Wednesday we nailed together some picnic tables and made final plans for a fire pit, where cooking for the multitude could be accomplished. That night my wife said not to worry, that a miracle had come to pass, that we were actually going to be ready. Almost.

On Thursday my parents arrived and later that day several others pulled in. By Friday morning the festivities were underway, and a carnival mood had spread throughout the homestead. There were children everywhere, each of them interested in his or her special thing.

"Can we go swimming yet?"

"Let's feed the chickens!"

"When do we eat again?"

"Can you give me a ride on your tractor?"

"What happens if we go down that trail past the barn?"

"Want Legos!"

And clustered around the kitchen table and out in the screen porch were the grownups, talking and laughing and generally catching up.

"So when did you start working there?"

"She just put her foot down, that's all. No more."

"And then the *baby* got sick, on top of everything else."

"Nahh! The Twins'll never catch up!"

"That's right. The manual says 5000, but I change it every 3000."

"So when are we going to eat?"

Hour by hour the magic seems to grow, so that the days and the nights take on a wonderful timeless quality, a sense of dreamlike beauty, and the words and laughter of the grownups and the shouts and giggles of the children wash back and forth through the woods as if caught in a wizard's spell, an enchantment that keeps sadness and death and the passing of time at bay, so that we can live intensely but effortlessly in this charmed and charming weekend reunion, each of us like cells reunited in the body of the family, brought together by some unvoiced urgency and caring.

No matter that the weather turns gray, unsummery. We carry our own sun inside.

At suppertime Saturday we build a big fire and into it and on it go foil-wrapped potatoes and ears of soaked corn and hamburgers and hot dogs and bratwursts, and later, in the darkness, the little ones roast marshmallows and make s'mores, and life is perfect and complete.

It doesn't matter now that tomorrow this gathering will end. What matters—all that matters—is that we are there right now, alive and laughing and loving.

The Bears and the Bees

T his spring, after years of careful deliberation, my wife and I became beekeepers.

Well, sort of.

I mean, we have bees, and we are trying very hard to take good care of them, so in that sense we are in fact beekeepers.

But when you factor in the bears, and consider who's done what to whom and when and why, the picture gets a little fuzzy.

It started out quite simply. (These sorts of things always start out simply.) We borrowed hive bodies and frames from a dear friend who has urged us for years to get into the hobby. We purchased bees from another friend, and from him borrowed two pamphlets on beekeeping. We sent away for a helmet and net and smoker and when they came we were feeling very good indeed. Our two boxes of bees were working their itzy-bitzy buns off hauling in pollen and nectar and multiplying their numbers at a dizzying rate.

Then came the bear.

Our son first noticed the damage, and informed us of same early on Sunday morning. We dressed and hurried up to the clearing where our colonies were housed—or had been. Instead of order there was mayhem. The hive boxes were strewn about, the tops knocked askew, and many of the frames were scattered about in various states of destruction. What bees remained buzzed about in anger and confusion, trying, it seemed, to make sense of something insane.

"What do you think?" I asked my wife.

"I think we should put things back together as best we can," she said. "They're dependent on us."

So we restored order to our little buzzing colonies, and after a few days things seemed clearly on the mend. But when the weekend returned, the bear did too, and this time his vandalism coincided with a heavy rain. Our bees, exposed to cold and water, suffered a grim reduction in numbers.

Depressed, we once again put things in order, vowing as we worked to put an end to the recurrent destruction. Asking around we were told the only workable defense was electric fencing. My sister, Beth, and her farmer husband, Tom, were kind enough to loan us a fencer. We assembled a protective palisade of posts and insulators around our bees—and before we cleared a path from the barn for the wire, the bear had struck again.

So now we're down to one hive box and the little colony inhabiting the box is once again faced with the need to build up its ranks. But the electric fence is very much complete and energized around the clock.

And it seems to be working, for how else could one explain the motivation that led our friend the bear to ransack our garbage cans last week? We've lived here for years, with never a garbage can mishap and suddenly—wham. I've got to believe it was an act of revenge, triggered by something shocking that happened up by the bees.

The Red Oak Tree

Scene of tree being felled. Growl of saw, spray of woodchips, creak of trunk as it begins to tilt, then swish and muffled crash as it topples into the snow. Sudden hole in the sky.

I stand looking up at the brilliant blue and then down at the fallen oak and I am filled with a strange mixture of exhilaration and remorse.

The tree is gone, and with it go a hundred other things. A squirrel's home. The living place of lichens. A resting branch for owls, for crows, for chickadees. A winter haven for a colony of carpenter ants. A hunting ground for woodpeckers. Shade for a dozen mammal species. Moisture, in the form of transpiration, for the shrubs and flowers and grasses that grew beneath its canopy. A living filter that trapped impurities from the air as the breeze moved the air across its many thousands of leaves. A vast recycling center that gathered expired carbon dioxide and reformed it into its constituent parts, so necessary for the lives of oxygen-breathers like ourselves. Acorns for fall and winter food. A living piece of sculpture whose shape and colors varied with the seasons. A buffer against the winter winds. And on and on and on, the functions and gifts so

Craig Nagel

numerous and so subtly interrelated that the brain groans at the task
of understanding.

For those of us stamped with the mindset of western culture, it's
comfortable and easy to think of the tree as something put here for
our use, period. But this narrow focus distorts the larger picture.

All life forms contribute to a greater whole. None exist alone,
disconnected from one another. The leaves of the tree interface with
the air, the roots with the soil, the root hairs with fungi and other
living organisms. When we kill a tree we kill a lot of other things,
too.

We humans are not separate from Mother Nature. To consider
us so is to admit a raging case of schizophrenia. We can no more
divorce ourselves from nature than we can exist apart from our own
bodies. When we cut into the tissue of life, whether with a chainsaw
or a scalpel or a bulldozer or a shotgun, we are bound to suffer pain,
for in an ultimate sense we are cutting into ourselves. All things are
related. But we can't quite admit that to ourselves. Like frenzied
surgeons, we have performed countless operations on old Mother
N., but we have not improved her health.

I stand by the fallen trunk and run my mittened hand over the
rough contours of its bark. I feel an urge to tell the tree I'm sorry. I
need its wood to ward away next winter's chill, but I am saddened
to have taken its life in order to continue my own.

Someday (soon, I hope) we will learn to take heat directly from
the sun, and so spare the lives of creatures as noble as this oak.

Narrative

Some thoughts come drifting in like ghosts from the past. The memory of Connie Matthieson's street rod. The way you accidentally drove a hard bargain down in Mexico. The fun to be had at auctions. The mysterious appearance of snow fleas. And others, more idea than memory, well up from some shadowy place inside and beg to be written down in order to be defined. An essay on fear, for example, or thoughts you have about craftsmanship.

Every so often, with deadline approaching, the writer dips into his mental wellspring only to find it dry. This is when you realize the truth of what Gene Fowler wrote some years ago: "Writing is easy: all you do is sit staring at the blank sheet of paper until the drops of blood form on your forehead." Fortunately, these moments don't occur too often, since intriguing topics abound. Once your mind fixes itself on a topic, things proceed more smoothly. As Sholem Asch observed, "It has been said that writing comes more easily if you have something to say."

Do I Hear Five?

My wife and I went to an auction the other day and came away convinced that, dollar for dollar, there are few things a person can do that bring more delight and entertainment.

We didn't go with the thought of buying anything in particular. Instead we went for the fun of it, just to be there. As usual, we had a fine time.

There is something very right and commonsensical about auctions, though not all of them are happy events. But even in the case of auction-as-last-resort, the thing itself is satisfying. I suppose in part it's the absence of hype and fancy packaging, a place where wares are displayed without embellishment or glamour, where you can buy a chair or some plates or a boat without going through the rigmarole of pretending that such purchases have anything to do with your status or sex appeal or inherent value as a human being.

But auctions are much more than mere places for moving the merchandise.

There are the smells. The musty odor of boxes full of aged *National Geographics*. The sickly-sweet whiff of cigar smoke drifting through the air. The alluring tang of sloppy joes cooking at the lunch wagon.

And the sounds. The staticky crackle of the auctioneer's amplifier, the hypnotic chant of his voice, the murmur of the crowd examining objects with an eye toward possible purchase.

And the sights. Ah, the sights. At auctions you see people, real people, of every imaginable size and shape and age and demeanor, wearing everything from Sunday finery to coveralls to thrice-patched jeans, with a decided prejudice toward the practical. I have stood at auctions next to older ladies wearing long johns beneath their dresses, and seen many a pair of feet clad in well-worn house slippers. You do a lot of standing around at auctions, and it makes sense to do your standing in comfort rather than pain.

Auctions are friendly events, filled with laughter and wisecracks and lots of good cheer (though I do recall one where a couple of old gents got fairly heated up disagreeing as to whether an antique headlight belonged to a Franklin or a Maxwell motorcar). There's some competition, of course, but even that tends to be good-natured, and if the bidding escalates into near warfare, well then the seller ends up getting a few more bucks.

Which, come to think of it, is the real beauty of auctions: they are win-win-win situations. The seller wins by getting rid of things he or she no longer needs or can afford; the buyer wins by getting something desired at a (generally) reasonable price; the auctioneer wins by getting a commission on the sales.

Whatever you call it, for the lover of auctions there is simply no thrill quite like the excitement of bidding on something that catches your fancy, of hearing the auctioneer working his rhythmic spell, of frantically trying to decide if the item is worth more than the last guy bid.

"Hey, we've got four we've got four I hear four that's a four give me five I need five give me five I say five give me five. Over there, you there, hup! Do I hear five?"

Street Rod

L ife is full of surprises.

Just about the time you think you've got it made, something falls apart. And just when you think you're ready to join the Over The Hill Gang, a flash of exhilaration illuminates your soul and you feel young again.

Such a flash struck me last week. I was sitting quietly, ignoring the ache in my hip, when out of nowhere I remembered Connie Matthieson's '36 Chevy.

I closed my eyes and floated back to 1959, my senior year of high school. It was just about this time of year, a crisp autumn evening, when this incredible car rumbled up to the hamburger joint where we used to hang out, and out of the car stepped Connie.

He walked with studied coolth, as if nothing unbelievable were happening, but in less than sixty seconds every booth in the place was vacated and we were all crowding around the Chevy. In the glow of the streetlights the car seemed to hover magically, its chrome work pulsing like kryptonite, its chopped body tensed upon the chassis like a wild thing waiting to pounce.

Through the babble of voices facts emerged. Yes, the car belonged to Connie, former mortal like the rest of us. No, it was not a gift. It was a labor of lengthy duration and great secrecy, finished only the day before. Yes, it was pretty much stock, except for certain items like the engine and transmission. No, the color was not black, it only looked so in the streetlights. It was in fact maroon, with a special kind of paint he said was called metallic.

So it went, with each guy feeling joy for good old Conrad and envy of an almost purple hue. Thing is, most of us were college bound. We were expected to put every spare nickel into the old college fund. No time and definitely no money for such frippery as rescuing a noble coupe from the junkyard and transforming it into a piece of rolling sculpture. No sir, we were expected to be sensible, even if it killed us. End of story.

And it was the end of the story, up until last week, when the flash occurred. I had gone my sensible way, gone on to college and then into the serious task of making a living, gone on through years of driving cars and trucks that were mostly tiresomely stock. No silliness here, other than a lyric interlude with a '53 MG roadster.

I do remember that Connie Matthieson died at a horribly early age, yet in his 20's. Just keeled over and passed away. And I do remember thinking at the time that maybe, somehow, he knew in some mystical way that he needed to go for the gusto when he did. But whether he knew it or not, he did in fact provide our gang with great vicarious joy, riding with him in a truly boss car, imagining in our daydreams that we too possessed magnificent machines.

Then, last week, the flash, and a guy far removed from teenhood gets to thinking. And thinking. And thinking.

Why not?

On Giving

Fall is gone. Winter impends. The days grow gray and sullen. The once flexible world turns brittle; mercy and ease retreat behind the ashen clouds.

But poking up into this foreboding time like the first flowers of spring come holidays, merry splashes of color and warmth. We join together, massing like birds before a storm, to share the feasts and give the presents, chasing the cold away with laughter and songs and lots of good talk.

True, traditions can enchain us, causing us to groan at the prospect of Uncle Fred's long-winded jokes or Aunt Tilly's foolish prattle. For some, the holidays act as depressants, heavy and laden with unsmiling obligation.

But within the thickets of empty ritual and dull routine the sap of joy and life still surges. It may be that all we have to do is prune away the dead and dying parts to let the meanings grow verdant again.

There is surely great wisdom in the placement and timing of these celebrations. Sleigh bells and snowflakes aside, Christmas would lose an important dimension if it were celebrated in July. The promise of redemption, the hope of rebirth, take on much greater significance when days are short and darkness dominates.

Similarly, the feast of Thanksgiving belongs right where it is on the calendar. There would be considerably less point in celebrating such an event in March or April or May. For it is the known harvest, not the speculative planting, that causes the table to groan; abundance proclaims that we shall make it through the lean months dead ahead.

There is, I think, a perfect rightness to these winter holidays, and an importance that can't be overstated. Nature nudges us this time of year to look inward and take stock. Now is the time for the counting of blessings, for the reckoning up of accounts. And it is no accident that these celebrations, one secular and one religious, are grounded in acts of sharing and giving.

It has long been known (and repeatedly forgotten) that the process of giving brings renewal and life to the giver. This is the message of all the prophets: at the root of love—at the root of life itself—is giving.

If traditions oppress, if commercialization threatens to overwhelm, if repetition all but renders you numb—well, then, give! Not of money only, or of tangibles. Far more important that we give of the heart, of the spirit. Time spent visiting someone old and housebound; time spent making a snowman with the kids; time spent scribbling the extra lines on the Christmas card to let the other person know you really care; these and hundreds of similar acts are the kind of giving that truly matters.

Nikos Kazantzakis, the writer and prophet from Crete, summarized it many years ago in a three-line poem:

"I said to the almond tree

'Sister, speak to me of God'

And the almond tree blossomed."

On Craftsmanship

This holiday season my mind became preoccupied with craftsmanship. Conversations with friends, the enjoyment of excellent food, and the delight of well-made gifts all conspired to fixate my thoughts on what goes into the process of doing a thing properly.

We are all, at times (and sometimes continuously), craftsmen. Any task, tiny or major, can be done in a variety of ways. When it is done with care and evident skill, it becomes a source of satisfaction to everyone. When it is done sloppily or without love, the result demeans us all.

The craftsman, I think, is an instrument through which beauty flows. He or she does not create beauty, but merely delivers it. The degree to which he succeeds depends on how finely tuned his mechanisms are. This is the craftsman's responsibility: to keep himself ready for the times when the potential for beauty may appear. Whether the job at hand is baking cookies or building a house, the result will depend on this readiness.

It is my conviction that the good, the true, and the beautiful are all manifestations of the same universal source. I don't believe it matters much whether we call the source God or Great Spirit or

Allah or Atman; these are merely human names. What does matter is that we recognize and respect and revere the source for inspiring (in-spiriting) the love and skill which we impart to the things we make.

It is difficult at times to see this connection between the spiritual and the mundane. In a technological world, the devices we use can block our view of the larger picture. Working with a computer may seem to involve little craftsmanship—but only because we are blinded to both the miracle of its existence and the fact that it enables us to do many things better and more cleanly than in days gone by. So it is with hundreds of other machines. Each is a tool—no more, no less—with which, if we choose, we can exercise craftsmanship and thereby participate in the cosmic urge toward order and beauty.

We are not born into a finished, static universe. The world at every level is an ongoing experiment, an unending quest for balance and harmony. From subatomic particles on up, everything fidgets and jiggles as it seeks a place of repose. The name of the game is to find a graceful fit: whether in human relations, international affairs, dressmaking, bookkeeping, or cabinetwork. Another word for this is craftsmanship.

The poet Kahlil Gibran once wrote that work is love made visible. By this, I think he meant to illuminate the hidden filaments that link us together with all of creation. The bird builds a nest; the oak puts out leaves and acorns; the star we call Sun radiates life-giving heat and light.

In like fashion, our work can be an outpouring of joy.

When it is, we are truly craftsmen—and truly at peace.

Hard Bargain

We were talking the other night about language, and about our first trip to Mexico many years ago to visit my sister, Carol, in Oaxaca.

Language is a thing we really don't think about much, like breathing. When we have something to say, we say it. If someone else says something, we listen. Since we all share a common tongue, there is no need to pay much attention to the language itself.

All of this changes when you go to a place where a different language is spoken.

In Mexico, for instance, people speak Spanish. Knowing this ahead of time, I was careful to prepare myself by learning a few basic words and phrases. With the help of my brother, Ricardo, a certifiable Spanish teacher, I memorized *si* (yes), *no* (no), *adios* (goodbye), *cerveza* (beer), and *baño* (bathroom), as well as the numbers from one to ten (except for six and seven, which I had some trouble with). Armed with this knowledge, I boarded a Mexicana Airlines 727 and flew to a point considerably south of the border.

The flight itself went smoothly, aside from the explanations given about the use of oxygen masks, which were evidently in Spanish, even when the flight attendant repeated them in English. Going through immigration was somewhat confusing when we changed planes in Mexico City, but then I suppose it always is, what with everyone being so tense.

But stepping out into the lobby of the airport in Oaxaca—holy *frijole*! All of a sudden people were speaking in tongues! Listening intently, I found that I could understand nothing. I stood around hoping someone would try talking to me, so that I could use some of my Spanish vocabulary, but nobody did. It was too early in the morning to order a beer and I didn't have to go to the bathroom, so there was nothing to do but listen, which I did to no avail.

Later, at the marketplace, I actually heard somebody say "*Buenos días*," which I remembered meant "Good morning." This gave my confidence a major boost, and I decided to try my hand at the Mexican national pastime, haggling (*regatear*). According to my sister, who has lived in Mexico for years and has actually learned to speak Spanish, the basic haggling strategy is to offer the seller half of the asking price and then work toward an agreement somewhere in between. But when a little old Indian lady came up to me offering a beautiful cotton shirt for twenty pesos, I couldn't remember the Spanish word for ten, so I said *no*. This caused her to speak very rapidly, pointing at the shirt and repeating *quince* over and over until, exasperated at not knowing what *quince* meant, I shook my head and said *no* again.

The lady rolled her eyes and muttered lots of words I didn't catch, and then she pointed at the shirt and said *diez*, which I suddenly remembered meant ten. "*Si!*" I cried, pulling out my wallet. "*Si! Si!*"

Later, when I asked my sister what *quince* meant, and found it was fifteen, I felt rather badly. It wasn't fair, after all, for an old pro like myself to have driven such a hard and merciless bargain.

Kickin' Back

We talked about it for months, ever since last summer.

Wouldn't it be nice to take a mid-winter vacation? Get away from the cold and the snow, go somewhere warm, lie on the beach, soak up some rays? We could log some meaningful hours of hammock time, restore our faded summer tans, sip multi-colored drinks sporting miniature beach umbrellas. And sleep. Ah yes. Sleep whenever the eyelids drooped, forget the alarm clock, snore until noon.

And maybe, once we regained our normal energies, we'd swim and snorkel and jog on the beach, rent a boat and catch some fish, maybe even try sailboarding or parasailing. What the heck. We'd be on vacation.

Weeks passed. The first frosts came and took our minds off gardening and lawn work, urged us to prepare for winter. Clean the chimney, check the snowplow, stack the firewood, stow all the summer gear. And still we talked. Where would be best? Florida? Mexico? The Bahamas? Belize? And when would be most satisfying? Right after Christmas? Mid-February? What about March?

Winter came and with it the joyful agony of preparing for all the holidays. Clean the house, cook the turkey, buy the presents, find a tree, decorate, send out cards, cook the ham, celebrate, collapse. The week after New Year's we felt like checking into rehab. But finally everything got back to normal and now it's time to make our move.

Or, shall I say, moves. In the plural.

Pick the time and place. Call the travel agent. Get on the Internet. Start making lists.

Who will we get to feed the cat? Water the plants? Check the heat?

Where are the passports? Are they still current? What about luggage? Everything there? And clothes. Warm-weather clothes. Does the old swimsuit still look okay? What about sandals? Short-sleeved shirts? Sunglasses? A hat of some kind, to guard against heatstroke? Oh, and sunscreen. And pills. And Band-Aids. And aspirin. And whatnot.

"Okay. Sure. We understand. If we fly out of Brainerd, we'll get in there too late to take the water taxi out to the island. No problem. We'll leave from the Cities."

"Honey, what's the name of that motel we stayed at with free shuttles to the airport? Yeah, that's right. We'll have to drive down there the night before."

Tick tick tick. The days evaporate. Who's gonna pick up the mail while we're gone? Plow the snow? Shovel the walk?

Did you change that dentist appointment? Tell the Andersons we can't come to dinner? Let the board know you won't be at that meeting?

And when we get back, we've got to remember to get the car oil changed right away, and get those birthday cards off in the mail, and order those seeds and that part for the lawn mower. Yeah, I know. We'll just have to work overtime, try to catch up. No, I didn't get sandals. Not yet. Or film. Or batteries for the camera and those forms for the tax return. I'll do it next week.

Nothing compares to the prospect of getting away.

What fun, to cast aside all cares and woes, step off the treadmill, relax.

They call it kickin' back.

The Some Days Never Come

I n John Steinbeck's masterful short novel *Of Mice and Men*, the two central characters, Lennie and George, share a dream of what life will be like in the future.

Each time the present becomes unpleasant or drained of hope, Lennie begs George to tell him "how it's gonna be." And George, though he knows better, complies.

"We'll have a cow," said George. "An' we'll have maybe a pig and chickens . . . and down the flat we'll have a . . . little piece of alfalfa—"

"For the rabbits," Lennie shouted.

"For the rabbits," George repeated.

"And I get to tend the rabbits."

"And you get to tend the rabbits."

Lennie giggled with happiness. "An' we'll live on the fatta the land."

This dream of the future sustains them both, even though they do nothing toward making it come true. Each time they're paid they fritter their money away, and because of Lennie's sub-normal intelligence, they are forever forced to move on to different jobs, until, near the end, Lennie accidentally kills someone and George, knowing the jig is up, holds a gun to the back of Lennie's head and prepares to pull the trigger.

But even then, as the vigilante gang is approaching and all hope of a future is gone, Lennie insists that George tell him "how it's gonna be."

This propensity of ours to dream of a better life, to wrap the unpleasantness of today in the swaddling clothes of an imagined tomorrow, is a universal one. Our ability to imagine may well be our most important survival tool.

But if we want to live as fully as we are able, we must look illusion in the face and admit the thing that George admits at the instant he pulls the trigger: the "some days" never come.

Never, that is, until we begin to work to make them happen.

Do you dream of a better way of life? Do you find yourself putting off what you'd really like to do because it doesn't seem practical right now? Do you feel incomplete, unhappy, unfulfilled?

Then you must take action, and commence to make the dreams come true. As Thoreau said, there is nothing wrong with castles in the air; that's where they belong. What we need to do is build real foundations under them.

Foundation-building can take many forms. For some, it may mean writing letters of inquiry about going back to school or searching for a different job. For others it might involve letting go of a house or car or other possession, the payments on which have proved to be too burdensome. Still others may need to join a twelve-step group to help overcome an addiction, or seek outside counsel in order to right or to end an unhappy relationship.

In the quiet of our own hearts, we know which aspects of our lives need improvement: our discontents and daydreams point the way. The danger lies in doing nothing; of drifting along under the narcotic spell of "some day."

Only when we set about underpinning our fantasies with real-life action can we hope to avoid the fate of Lennie and George. If we don't take steps to make our dreams come true, they won't.

Without steadfast effort on our part, the *some days* never come.

Waiting For Spring

People who live in cold climates spend a lot of time waiting for spring.

It's not that winter isn't fun. If you didn't like winter, you'd move someplace warm. Whether you're the outdoor type or the kind who likes getting comfy with a good book, winter brings with it an undeniable magic. The first snowfall transforms a drab landscape into a place of wonder. Sunshine refracts into jewels. The formation of ice allows you to walk upon water. Passing animals stitch visible tracks into the quilting of snowflakes. Jack Frost etches intricate scenes upon your window glass. Sounds grow muffled. Breath becomes visible. The drifts of frozen crystals enable you to slide and ski and sled over the otherwise restraining earth.

Old Man Winter has his charms. But there comes a point, sometime between Christmas and Easter, when you'd prefer him to be gone. "Enough!" you cry. "That's long enough! You're hogging more than your fair share of months!" So you start waiting for spring. Having shifted mental gears, you begin to notice clues that would otherwise be overlooked. A five-degree rise in temperature. The lusty cavorting of hormone-drenched squirrels. A cacophony of crows. The faint greening of popple tree bark.

Spying such signs, you grow bolder. The midafternoon drip of icicles sets you to whistling. A full day of sunshine triggers thoughts of vernal tasks: washing windows, painting trim, tilling the garden plot. A three-day thaw confirms your rising hopes. It won't be long now. Spring is just around the corner.

Then it snows. You frown. A minor setback. You grab the shovel and clear the sidewalk one more time. You give yourself a pep talk to bolster your flagging spirits. No worries. It's just a matter of time.

Then it snows again, and the temperature plummets. Dark thoughts assail your weary mind. You remember the careless way you dismissed pre-Christmas thoughts of going to Maui in March. You drag the shovel out and grudgingly clear the walk.

And so the cycle goes. Like swimmers caught in a riptide, we ride a swelling wave in toward the shore of spring, only to find ourselves flung backward by outrushing currents.

We struggle, too, against other, larger forces. We long to regain unblemished health, to retain unflagging vigor. We dream of enduring love, of opportunities not bungled. We link perfection and prosperity and peace of mind with an imagined spring, and look with sullen eyes upon the flawed reality of who we are today.

But today is all we really have, and we are foolish not to live it fully. Today we are alive and know it; tomorrow is, in truth, conjecture, probable but not guaranteed.

It's natural to long for spring. But it's a mistake to put our lives on hold while waiting for the future. Today the snow may come again, further frustrating our yearnings. This day may find us compromised, incomplete, not quite ready. And that's okay.

Today is a wonderful day to be alive.

The Skeptic and the Snow Fleas

Ignorance dies slowly.

For hundreds of years after Galileo proposed that the earth circled the sun, most folks "knew better."

Scarcely more than a century ago, taking a bath was considered bad for one's health.

And last week a friend of mine laughed disrespectfully when I tried to explain about snow fleas. "Sure," he said. "Of *course* there are little black fleas that jump around in the snow. I believe you. Tell me—are they related to those rabbits you see in a bar now and then, the ones with the antlers?"

I tried to stay civil. "No, I don't think so. The funny rabbits—jackalopes—are mere taxidermical tricks. Snow fleas, on the other hand, are real. They come out when the temperature gets just above freezing. But they're really small, like specks of black pepper. The only reason you can see them at all is because they hang around together in big swarms."

"I see. Um hmm. Great big swarms, eh?"

"OK. *Little* swarms then. And the swarms vary in size. The smallest I've seen was as big as your hand. The largest was maybe the size of a pizza."

My friend nodded sagely. "Ah, yes. A pizza. Tell me—do you ever have weird dreams?"

Sensing skepticism on his part, I deftly changed the subject to genealogy and offered hints regarding the nature of his family tree and the deformation of some of its branches. Then I absented myself from his sputtering presence and went directly to my encyclopedia.

There I found that snow fleas belong to a group of small (minute to one-fifth inch) primitive wingless insects known as springtails, so called because many species possess appendages under the abdomen which can be forced down and back, thus catapulting the insects into the air.

Springtails, I found, are widely distributed, ranging from the Antarctic to the Arctic, and are abundant, though often unobserved, in moist plant debris. "Certain springtails known as snow fleas are active at near-freezing temperatures and may appear in large numbers on snow surfaces." Springtails belong to the order *Collembola*, and usually feed on decaying vegetable matter or fungi, though occasionally they attack living plants. The young hatch from spherical eggs and closely resemble the adults.

I closed the encyclopedia and thought about my friend. Poor fellow. Just think what he's missing. And right at that stage of winter when every diversion is most welcome. If only he could set aside his skepticism and go out and look!

There on the south-facing banks he would see them, minuscule smudges of soot upon the sparkling white of the snow, a jiggling mass of itty-bitty life, dancing and leaping as if to welcome spring.

Narrative

The craft of journalism is based on the idea of keeping track of what happens. At the heart of the word "journalism" lies the word "journal," meaning "daily," as in the French phrase *du jour*, derived from the Latin *diurnalis*, "of the day." A journalist, then, in the narrowest sense, is one who keeps a journal, or record of each day.

What motivates someone to keep such a record? From what I've gathered through a lifetime of reading and talking with other writers, I'd say it comes down to having at least a mild obsession about the passage of time. A writer is someone who's unwilling to let his or her life go past without making note of the fact. Maybe the need to keep track of things is no different from that which impels the graffiti artist: the urge to scribble some sort of "Kilroy was here" on the walls of time. It's a way, I suppose, of tracking the invisible; of drawing footprints beneath the unseen movement of the years.

One of the delights of writing a recurring column is the freedom you have to poke into all sorts of corners. As an example, the next few essays explore a variety of topics: our relationship to time, musings about gravity, what happens when we get serious about taking good care of something, and why some people seem to retain a childlike sense of wonder into adulthood, while others don't.

Keeping Time

A few years ago we inherited a clock, thanks to the kindheartedness of a dear aunt. The clock originally belonged to my dad's mother, and dates from the early 1900's. It came to us carefully packed in a good strong box, and when we opened the box we could hardly believe our eyes.

"It's beautiful!" said my wife.

"It's big!" said I.

"It's old!" said she.

"And it doesn't use batteries!" (Having once spent an unholy several days sanding and refinishing a wood floor spattered with black spots from a leaking clock battery, I long ago hardened my heart against such contemporary conveniences. Besides, batteries cost money.)

"So how does it run?" asked our daughter.

"With this!" I said, holding forth a large metal key. "It's a wind-up job."

Our daughter wasn't very impressed. "What if you forget to wind it up?"

"The spring runs down and it stops," I explained. "Then you reset it and wind it up again and you're back in business. Piece of cake."

And so it was that the old clock came into our lives. My wife applied elbow grease and paint stripper to the woodwork, and transformed it from a dark and dated looking thing into a genuine eye-grabber. Standing nearly two feet high and measuring a foot in width, the old clock now dominates the top of our piano. Its intricately carved cabinet glows a rich reddish brown in the ambient light, and the glass door with its semicircle top and frosted scene of two herons and a pond delights all who look upon it.

True, it didn't exactly *work* when we first tried to make it go. But we took it to the clock-repair experts at our local jewelry store, and a few days later the mechanical parts were good as new. "They said it's a seven-day clock," said my wife. "And that it would probably work just fine for another 90 years."

Thus it was that we became keepers of time. If we want the joy of our old clock's *ticktock*, we have to remember to wind it. If we want to glance at the Roman-numeraled face and get a correct fix on the time, we have to remember to wind it. If we want to hear the reassuring *bong* of its chimes, we have to remember to wind it.

All of which has subtly changed our relationship to time itself. Time is no longer something that happens without us. If we want to keep track of time, we have to remember to wind the clock.

Sure, once or twice we've gotten rebellious and just let it run down and stop. But after a day or two we get to missing the rhythmic ticking as the old machine measures out the days, and soon the key is applied and the heart of the venerable corpse ratchets back to life, to meter out the moments and add grace and beauty and a gentle sense of fitness to our home.

Moon Thoughts

Standing outside staring at the full moon, I felt a powerful yearning to go visit it.

With a gravitational force one-sixth as strong as the earth's, the moon must be an ideal place for dancing, or for track or field events. A 60-pound child would weigh 10 pounds up there; a 120-pound lady a mere 20; guys like me a buoyant 30+ and easily able to outjump your average NBA star.

Aside from cavorting around, the moon would be an excellent location for people in my line of work. Being a stonemason means you have a rather adversarial relationship with gravity. But think how easy things would be up on the moon. A spine-straining sack of cement would shrink to the weight of a bowling ball and a concrete block would be no heavier than your lunch bucket.

Farmers, think how painless it would be to toss hay bales onto the wagon! You'd get so you could hardly wait for haying time to come again. Appliance dealers would flip refrigerators around like empty cartons. Loggers would throw saw logs effortlessly onto their trucks. Piano movers would giggle.

There would, of course, be drawbacks to living a lunar life. Chiropractors would be out of business. Sumo wrestlers would have to gain weight. Skinny fashion models would have to buy lead shoes so they wouldn't drift up into space. No doubt the advertising wizards would turn to emphasizing heavy: Don't Be An Air Belly—Drink Coors Ponderous.

But the advantages would predominate.

Clumsy folks would gain a deft touch. Depressives would grow lighthearted. Shot ducks would glide gracefully down into the water. Hippos would tiptoe about, secretly dreaming of forming ballet troupes.

In time, though, I suppose we'd adjust to the feather-light conditions and begin to complain all over again. Just as the astronauts have trouble downing liquids in weightless conditions, we'd no doubt find lunar liberation irksome. As the old adage warns, beware what you wish for lest it come true.

Wonderful as it seemed to me standing in the darkness gazing at the distant moon, I realized upon reflection that living up there would probably be no great improvement. Cement manufacturers would simply make much bigger bags; bales of hay would grow sixfold; insurance underwriters would scale up the ideal-weight tables; and we'd be right back where we started from.

Maybe the limits we have here on earth aren't so bad. Maybe it's better that hippos move slowly and harbor no dreams of donning tutus. Maybe it's best to accept things as they are and learn to use our limitations as helpful guides.

But it's still fun to stare into space and wonder.

Tending the Patch

For many years I was a grower of raspberries.

From the first greening of the canes in early spring on through the running of berry juice down the chin, I faithfully pruned and hoed and mulched and watered, eager to see what our little patch would yield.

Then I fell behind, a victim of busyness, and the raspberry patch declined. Weeds invaded the once-clean rows. Dead canes stood bleak against the sky. Gophers remodeled the shape of the land, causing pimples of raw dirt to erupt on the face of the carefully groomed terrain.

Had my neglect continued much longer, the beloved patch would have been lost. But one day I wandered over to this site of former glory and felt a surge of sadness and self-disgust. I stood there for quite awhile, clouded with negative thoughts. A bitter taste rose in my throat. Best just to plow it all under. Best to admit the ugly truth of my own laziness. Best just to walk away and let it become a memory.

And then I got mad.

The next night I went to work. A shovel, powered by anger, made short work of the gopher mounds. A pruning shears attacked the dead canes. Scratches bloodied my arms, fair penance to pay for my long neglect. By the end of the evening the garden cart was heaped with culled canes and the patch looked more like a place for life than death.

The following night I started pulling weeds. Inch by inch I worked my way down the rows, clearing the ground of all but raspberry plants. Dandelions, wild strawberries, clumps of grass, tendrils of vetch—all came out of the ground and went into the cart. It was not easy work. But the further I went, the more determined I became to make the little patch a place of neatness and order and health. When, at length, I straightened from my labors and surveyed the results, I could see that great headway had been made.

That weekend I went to the nursery and bought some new plants to fill in the holes in the rows. When I was done putting them in, the patch looked better than it had in years.

Later, standing with the hose and spraying much-needed water on the thirsty patch, I realized it was not only the plants I was helping, but also myself.

There is, I saw, a vast satisfaction that comes from getting a portion of your life in excellent order. The object of your efforts can be anything: restoring an old car, learning a new craft, embarking on a program of physical fitness, setting up a workshop, putting in a flower garden, getting all your photos organized. It doesn't matter what you do, so much as that you *do* it.

We complain that life is too hurried, too superficial, too complex. I submit that the antidote is to make portions of our lives into oases of pure excellence.

The more of ourselves we attend to, the more of ourselves will bear fruit.

Ready or Not

Each day, it seems, the mail includes another graduation announcement.

Seeing them pile up on the desk makes me aware of how quickly the years go by and how short a time childhood is.

Can these near-adults really be the same little critters I saw squirming around in playpens just a few years back? How, pray tell, can this metamorphosis have occurred? Has someone been tampering with the clock or tearing pages from the calendar when I'm not around?

And how is it possible that these young folks can be judged educated and ready to face the world on their own?

Clearly they cannot be ready. I know, from the vantage point of further years, that they are not. It's folly to presume that a mere dozen years of school can prepare anyone for the buffeting that lies ahead.

No, they are not ready to live as adults. Most adults are barely ready for it. We pretend to be because we haven't any choice—but deep down most of us know how childish we actually are.

Yet life roars on. When you're 17 or 18 you want to *proceed* with things. The whole world's out there waiting to be experienced and explored. And it's basically a friendly world, awash with promise and the prospect of adventure.

So the skeptic with his mounting pile of graduation mail mutters to himself and thinks some more. He walks back in memory and revisits the scenes of his own life's major events.

Was he, at the time, really ready to step out of high school and go on to college? He was not.

Was he, some few years later, actually ready to enter the mystery of marriage? He was not.

Was he fully prepared to bring new life into the world and to nurture and guide it wisely? He was not.

Nor was he truly prepared for being a soldier, or later a teacher, or later yet a journalist. He knew in his bones he was not. But each time he did it, managed it, made it work in spite of the hard parts—or maybe because of them.

Reflecting on this, I began to see things differently. If, as teachers repeatedly point out, education is the process not of filling in but of drawing out, then maybe the question of being prepared is irrelevant.

Maybe instead you learn as you go, grow as you face obstacles, get toughened and sharpened and toned by the poundings and pummelings life sends your way. And maybe it's best just to dive into things, ready or not, trusting that somehow you'll learn to swim.

This I know: education is a process, not a package, and it goes on and on and on until the day you die, and possibly thereafter.

Twelve years of classroom work is merely the beginning, a sort of warm-up time before the main event.

So jump on in and join us, graduates.

The water's just fine.

A Sense of Wonder

An old friend and I went for a long walk the other day, and while we walked we talked about how people act and how their actions affect one another.

On the negative side, it's easy to see how anger or bitterness can ripple right through an entire group. The general has a bad day on the golf course and reprimands the colonel; the colonel barks at the major; the major chews out the captain; the captain dresses down the lieutenant who reams out the sergeant who screams at the private who kicks the company dog.

In the simplest of schemes, we transfer emotion to one another like a toppling line of dominoes. And negative emotions, my friend and I decided, have an almost gravitational force in that they insist on pulling their way down through amazingly long lines of people.

Where these feelings originate is not entirely clear. Why, on a given day, might a disagreement with your spouse turn into something ugly, when the day before you might have ended laughing? Is the fountainhead enzymatic, a little trickle of chemicals in the cells? And whence cometh depression, that most modern of maladies? Is the source of this widespread condition mainly molecular? Or is it the spirit, downtrodden, that in turn infects the body with its woes?

How, we wondered, walking along, can a nation so favored and so formidable as ours be so shot through with hateful disagreements? Are we, deep down, beginning to run scared? How have we come to be more concerned with touting our rights than with telling right from wrong? Are we infecting one another with some weird emotional virus, a spiritual counterpart to AIDS?

And how is it possible ever to feel bored in a world so brimming with marvels?

"I suppose," said my friend, "that it all comes down to whether or not you have a sense of wonder. If you believe the universe is miraculous, you'll find life exciting and always discover new things to learn and do. And if you don't, you won't."

But where, I wondered, does the awareness of majesty come from? Is it something taught to you in infancy? Or does it arise of its own accord inside each of us, only to be gradually eroded for some by the difficulties that rain down upon us? Why do certain people see the glass of life as being half-full while others see it as half-empty while still others vibrate with excitement at the fact that the glass contains anything at all?

We know in our bones that enthusiasm matters. With it, the drab and humdrum grow colorful and vibrant. The word itself comes from the Greek roots *en theos*, meaning god-inspired, having a god in you, or being in the presence of a god. Sadly, the fact that our enthusiasm waxes and wanes without conscious choice on our part makes clear that we can't control it.

At root, the source remains a mystery. We are born; we totter about the earth for X number of years; we die. But I do believe my friend is right.

In between the start and the stop a lot depends on our capacity for wonder.

Sweet Summertime

There's something about the textures of summer that makes you remember the days of your youth.

The trickle of sweat running down your side, the tang of a just-picked tomato, the night sounds of crickets and tree frogs and billions of bugs—all conspire to hurtle you back through the years to the summers when you were a kid.

Back then, summers lasted. From the frantic chants of "School's out, school's out, teacher let the monkeys out" on through the majestic blue-sky mornings when you stepped outside barefoot and felt the dew-damp grass between your toes, to the occasional ecstasy of a tree-snapping, duck-drowning, ripsnorter of a thunderstorm, summer rolled on and on and on, a great comforting river of time, so long and so wide and so embracing that worries disappeared around the bend.

Summer seemed a magic time, a strange dimension in which even the pull of gravity was lessened. Maybe it had to do with trading in your school shoes for a pair of sneakers. Suddenly you felt much lighter, capable of running faster and jumping longer and climbing higher than you thought possible. Or maybe it was just that gravity-laden adults receded into the background and, along with other kids, you were free to soar.

Whatever the reasons, summers were wonderful back then. The real you (not the school-year you) emerged from its chrysalis of responsibility and took to skipping down the lane. Away from the all-seeing eyes of teachers and parents, you took the hooligan path of petty thievery, laziness, and moral lassitude. A melon stolen from the neighbor's garden tasted honey sweet. Sneaking off before your chores were finished felt so good it made you nervous. Sitting hidden in the tree branch pretending not to hear your mother calling made you shiver with delight.

And the projects and the ballgames and the dreams! Lord, it was all so exciting and so twitchy-nerve alive, so rounded and ongoing and perfect.

I remember the summer we built the raft and poled it, half-submerged, down the channel that ran to Mud Lake. And how we built the soapbox racers, scouring the dump for buggy wheels and tin cans to mount on the orange-crate hoods as headlights. And the care we lavished on the Indian camp, a dozen huts of bent saplings thatched with meadow grass, and the ring of rocks for the council fire, and the homemade bows and arrows so patiently crafted we found they could puncture skin at a distance of ten paces.

There was an innocence built into those summers of yore. Granted, there was also some poor judgment, as you found out when you came back home to your unfinished chores. And it's true that smoking corn-silk tobacco is not provocative of health. But we hadn't learned that overexposure to sunlight could cause cancer, so we all turned ten shades darker and felt extremely well, and if questioned as to what a lawsuit was, we'd probably have figured it was something worn by a judge.

Then we'd have put such nonsense out of mind and gotten back to the important things, like working more neat's-foot oil into the baseball mitt or digging up some worms with which to tantalize the bluegills, secure in the knowledge that summer was forever.

Narrative

L ike many of our neighbors here in the woods, we learned to do a variety of things to help insure our survival. Shortly after purchasing our land, we enrolled it in the Tree Farm program and, with the aid of area foresters, developed a management plan to help guide decisions about the use and well-being of our woods. Over the ensuing years we cut dozens of mature pines for building material and hundreds of birch, aspen, and oak for firewood. We planted several thousand seedlings of various species, cut and maintained walking trails around the property, had a pond dug in the lowland as a watering place for wildlife and an ice skating rink for ourselves, and generally tried to work with the natural inclinations of the land and the other life forms that grew upon it.

Though we lived frugally, we managed to take several trips: to Maine, to Texas, to Washington and Oregon, and to several points in between. The kids were growing like weeds and becoming an ever-greater delight. We played lots of baseball, made frequent jaunts to the lake to swim and fish, hunted grouse in the fall, learned to cross-country ski in the winter, read countless books, and worked at improving the house and grounds. The only thing that didn't pan out was significant income from my writing. Instead I threw my energies into masonry work.

Weary of spending hours at the desk, I found the switch to physical work delightful. I've always loved to work with my hands and to build things, and the chance to grow ever more competent at the craft of masonry brought lots of satisfaction. Then, too, the opportunity to build strength and fitness while making an income seemed an uncommon bonus.

I decided to focus on building fireplaces. I read voluminously and asked endless questions of other masons and material suppliers. In my readings I came across a book about Benjamin Thompson, an early American inventor and contemporary of Benjamin Franklin who picked the British side during the revolution and ended up moving to Europe, where he earned the title Count Rumford and made a name for himself converting ill-drawing fireplaces to functional health by changing the size and shape of the firebox. In time his improved models came to be known as Rumford heaters, and proved to be considerably better at radiating heat and conserving fuel than conventional models or the famous stove invented by Franklin. I couldn't wait to build my first Rumford, and followed Thompson's ratios with extreme care. When it proved a success, I knew I was on the right track, and over the subsequent decades built dozens of them.

At first, many of the jobs we did were built of brick. But little by little customers began requesting bids involving stonework. More research revealed the fact that the indigenous stone found in north-central Minnesota had been moved here by successive glaciers, and was originally part of a vast mountain range north of what is now Lake Superior. Radiometric dating shows our stone to be among the oldest on the planet, with some of it having been formed some two to nearly three billion years ago. It has also proved to be quite beautiful when broken open, with colors ranging across the spectrum from the white of quartz to the black of basalt. I bought an old splitting maul and began learning to split stone, which proved to be slow going and hard on the back and shins. Eventually I took the plunge and bought a large hydraulic rock splitter and expanded my operation to include selling split stone to other area masons. Over time we found ourselves splitting and selling or installing several hundred tons of stone per year.

The Eye of God

Several years ago a pair of chipmunks established residency under the concrete slab of our screened porch.

Ma and Pa quickly set about producing offspring, their actions driven by an ancient rodent wisdom: the more of us there are, the greater our chances of survival.

And survive they did, down to the present generation of high-octane tremblers that dart and chatter as if powered by nitrous oxide. You'd think moving at the speed of dragsters would eventually prove counterproductive, sending many to the rocking chair prematurely to nurse their worn-out joints. Maybe it does. Were their burrow roofed with glass instead of concrete, maybe you'd see long lines of the infirm rocking away.

But speed, as any observer will tell you, is not the only trick up the chipmunk's furry sleeve.

There's also paranoia.

Chipmunks are always on guard. Like their cousins the red squirrels, chipmunks proceed through life by fits and starts. First a moment's wary survey of surroundings, then a lightning dash ahead, followed by a freeze-frame minute of distrustful stillness, and a final breakneck blur to safety. It's as if their minds alternate between spells of manic high and depressive low, with each state lasting only seconds before giving way to its opposite.

But perhaps these observations do no justice to the harried chipmunk. They are, after all, derived from the human perspective, and may grossly differ from the rodent's-eye view. Which brings up the interesting question as to whether any species can ever begin to understand another.

Towering several feet above this bundle of quivering fur, I see his world as simple and quaint.

Instead of preparing himself with lengthy schooling followed by meaningful employment with a reputable firm, the chipmunk limits his vocation to a search for nuts, seeds, and berries. In place of solemn vows and an effort at lifelong monogamy, this critter zips through the mating ritual and gets right at the business of procreation. Eschewing the purchase of land and the drawing up of a long-term mortgage, he widens the tunnel to the hole under my cement and calls it home.

Seen through my godlike eyes, his frantic speed and paranoid fears seem amusing, his sense of self-importance laughable, his view of reality limited in the extreme. Then a different thought assails me, and my knowing smile darkens into a frown.

Seen through the eyes of a Higher Power, how must we humans appear?

Miss Patience

Our dog's name is Bonny. She's an English springer spaniel, brown and white, and over a decade old.

Like most springers, she's full of enthusiasm. If you return from an absence of, say, ten minutes, she wags her hindquarters so vigorously you fear she'll dislocate her spine. Walk toward her with a treat and she positively trembles. Let her outside after being cooped up for the night and she'll tear around in circles like a teenager spinning donuts in a gravel parking lot with his first truck.

This superabundance of energy has its downside. Trying to get her to sit quietly for more than five minutes is close to impossible. Taking her for a ride to the vet means risking your life. Asking her to stay near you as you walk through the woods is futile; she'll obey for a minute at best, or less if she crosses an interesting scent. (Knowledgeable readers will note that we missed a few vital lessons during the early training months.)

Given Bonny's reckless lust for life, I've always thought of her as lacking patience. True, she'll spend hours trotting about the property, nose to the ground, sniffing the hip-hop trail of a vanished rabbit. I'll also grant that she has never tired of playing with visiting kids.

105

But in the main she's hyperactive, zipping about as if some mad surgeon had implanted a pacemaker inside her and programmed it to beat at twice the normal speed.

Then one day I watched her through the window as she sat waiting outside for my wife to take her for a walk. Minutes passed as two incoming phone calls kept the walk on hold. A squirrel, blocked by Bonny from access to the bird feeder, crept gingerly around behind her. Chickadees fluttered about her head. A woodpecker dislodged a tasty morsel from the suet block, which rolled down the snowbank to stop at Bonny's side. Through all of these tempting distractions she sat immobile, eyes fixed on the window, waiting for her friend.

I began to recall other instances of patience, some of long duration. If Bonny sleeps outside in her straw-bale hut, which she prefers to do when the night's not too frigid, she wakes at the sound of coffee brewing and trots around to the front door, awaiting her morning treat. How long will she wait? The record so far is nearly half an hour. If, in the summer, she chases a chipmunk into a hidey hole, she'll sit stock-still for countless minutes waiting for it to pop back out. Should she flush a grouse when we're out walking, she'll lock into a point and stay there till we walk on past.

Or take the matter of smells. She must feel like a college professor trying to teach a preschooler the ABC's when it comes to deciphering scents. Imagine her frustration when I, a crudely calibrated human barely able to distinguish between Chanel No. 5 and sweat socks, blunder unknowingly past the delicate spoor of a tunneling shrew or the exquisite hint of decaying raccoon scat.

Little by little I've come to revise my thinking. Maybe I'm the impatient one. When I think of the hundreds of mornings she's kept her dignity while in agony to get outside and relieve herself, or the dozens of evenings we've gone off visiting, leaving her not knowing when—or even if—we're coming back, I feel a bit uneasy.

We proud masters of such lowly canines don't like being humbled. We were bred for other loftier positions. But maybe, just maybe, we could learn something here. Or, failing that, spend a few weeks in obedience school, brushing up on patience.

Reclining Years

The stages of life are few and heartless: birth, youth, maturity, decline, death. We whisk from cradle to casket like travelers trapped on a runaway train, muttering to ourselves the age-old question: "Vyizzit ve grow too soon oldt und too late schmart?"

Fellow passengers, take heart.

There is hope.

By applying my creative powers to the problem at hand, I have hit upon a way to lessen our grief and remove some of the sting from the too-soon/too-late dilemma.

It all started with a furniture ad.

There on the page in living color was the Millennium Recliner, an oversized beauty replete with an insulated pocket for cold beer, a built-in TV remote, and a switch to make the whole thing vibrate.

My heart raced, as did my mind. These guys were on to something! Only trouble was, they hadn't taken the concept far enough.

Tumultuous thoughts cascaded through my brain. The words of the seventeenth-century poet George Herbert bubbled from memory: "Living well is the best revenge." Aha! Of course. You can't stop the aging process, but you can sure as hell make it less painful. The key is to coddle. Wrap yourself in pleasure. Indulge.

I thought back to the pitiless phases of life and saw in a flash that between maturity and decline, one could insert a new stage: recline.

Ideas poured from my fevered head like quarters from a winning slot machine. To maximize the joy of your reclining years, you'd need to feel perpetually warm and fuzzy. I grabbed a pencil and paper and printed DESIGN SPECS in big block letters and set to work.

Warm and fuzzy implied heat and a sensuous fabric. No problem. I wrote "built-in electric blanket/heating pad" and "upholster with baby-blanket type material, to include attached comforter(s) for covering legs and feet. Satin edging optional."

I closed my eyes and imagined relaxing in such a chair. Old lullabies played in my mind and I felt myself swaying from side to side. I opened my eyes and the pencil raced over the paper. "Build stereo speakers into headrest with volume controls on console." "Install multiple motion-producing devices in chassis—rocking, jiggling, swaying, etc., with appropriate toggles on console."

Such things would require a motor. So why not put the whole thing on wheels, couple a belt to a small drive shaft, add a tiller or steering wheel, and go for broke? I scribbled as fast as I could, but the torrent of ideas threatened to outrace my pencil.

Thoughts of mobility led on to food. Just drive the recliner to the kitchen, stock up, and return to the TV. I wrote down "built-in fridge" and "built-in microwave" and "built-in sink (small)" and "modest cabinetry with utensils and tableware for one." The concept of an on-board sink led naturally to thoughts of plumbing, which in turn led on to the notion of a built-in toilet or waste-disposal unit, a la the astronauts. If they could do it in a rocket, why not in a recliner?

I clicked the pencil against my teeth and quivered with excitement. The ultimate cocoon! And why not solar powered? I wrote down "embed photovoltaic panels in exterior sides and roof" and "park next to window to recharge for night use." And still my mind raced on.

"On-board laptop computer."

"Headset telephone with pager and retractable mike."

"Foldout copier/fax/scanner in armrest opposite console."

"Small bookshelf/magazine rack."

"Built-in back scratcher."

"Male/female personal grooming articles, i.e., hairbrush, razor, toothbrush, cosmetics, etc., with swing-out mirror and lights."

I put the pencil down, knowing it was time to give my head a rest. Too much of this could lead you to delirium. I stood up and stretched, aware of knotted muscles. The idea of an all-purpose recliner was great, but what about getting exercise?

Then it dawned, and I added a final line to the list of specifications. "Build treadmill into footrest, so occupant can keep active while enjoying other entertainments."

And there you have it.

The Ultracliner.

Patent pending.

The Cutting Edge

Like you, dear reader, I prefer to think of myself as reasonably savvy and up-to-date.

Others may fall behind the times and grind along repeating things that have been outmoded—but not you and I. People like us stay up-to-the-minute, living life on the cutting edge.

Take, for example, lawn care.

Many years ago I cut grass with a reel-type push mower propelled purely by human power. The mower had once belonged to my grandfather, who lived in Chicago on a rather small lot. When Gramps moved into an apartment he bequeathed the mower to my father, who showed no interest in using it. Thus it was handed to me.

It made a satisfying *snick-snick-snick* when you got it moving fast enough, but usually it jammed up with crabgrass and pulled the stuff out by the roots, leaving unsightly craters in the lawn. When, in later, more sophisticated years, I took up the game of golf, I was delighted to learn that the technical name for such a crater is actually "divot." Later yet, when in disgust I retired from the game, it was largely because of divots. That, and a persistent slice. But I digress . . .

Fast forward through the years. Technology marches on, putting ever more sophisticated equipment into the eager hands of lawn tenders. The gas rotary mower. The self-propelled gas rotary mower. The riding mower. The weed whacker. The electric mower. The tractor and bush hog.

Decade after decade we rushed to buy the latest instruments available to give us the advantage in our unceasing battle with the turf. These sophisticated weapons did not come cheap. But who can measure the thrill that surges through your warrior soul when, sweaty and battle worn, you look down in triumph at the fallen enemy, each of his blades shorn off at a uniform height, so vanquished he'll not rise for at least another week.

And yet, and yet.

Through the years doubts crept in. Is this battle worth fighting? Is all the weaponry worth the cost? What about spending some hours in a hammock?

The uncertainties started decades ago when, as a GI stationed in Germany, I showed photos of our American house to some German friends.

"What's the flat stuff in front?" they asked.

"Our lawn," I said. "Grass."

"For what?"

"To look at, I guess."

"Do you harvest it?"

"We cut it, yeah. Every week or two."

"What do you feed it to? Cattle?"

"No. It's not for food."

"Then why do you have it? Wouldn't you be better off growing flowers or something to eat?"

Try as I might, I couldn't explain the rationale behind having and tending a lawn. In a part of the world where land is scarce and grasses are reserved for grazing sheep, lawns make little sense.

Now, decades later, I've come full circle.

Why bother cutting so much grass? Why not just cut a few spots here and there, large enough to keep the bugs down but small enough to give you hammock time?

Think about it. A cutting-edge concept, my friends.

Just say "no" to lawn care.

But What Do You Do?

"**B**ut what do you do?"

It's a very common question. Usually the asker is a city person come to visit someone in the woods. After an initial day oohing and aahing about the peace and serenity of country life, the question begins working its way toward the asker's lips.

"It certainly is quiet out here. And you mean to tell me you don't lock your doors at night? Boy, that's something. Down our way we wouldn't dare leave the house unlocked. Or the car either. But tell me . . . what do you do around here? I mean, for entertainment."

Whereupon, depending on his circumstances and how long he has lived in the country, the host begins a rambling and generally apologetic explanation about how, really, there are all sorts of things to do here in the boondocks. He mentions things like listening to music and reading books and browsing the Internet. He talks rhapsodically about fishing, perhaps, or golf, or grouse hunting, and his wife interjects about walking in the woods and feeding the birds and gardening. But sooner or later the conversation tends to peter out, and the host and his guest are left with certain doubts.

For both the city man and his country counterpart tend to measure entertainment by its packaged, advertised, consumer value.

And though the country man knows in his bones he has nothing to feel ashamed about, still he feels vaguely unsure. Is he actually missing out on something by not living closer to civilization? Is life in the city not richer and more exciting?

The answer, of course, is that it can be, depending upon what gladdens your heart. Obviously, major museums, top-flight concerts, forty-acre malls, and major-league ball parks will not be found in the country. Nor will congestion, frenzy, or the prospect of drive-by shootings. The key thing is what brings you satisfaction.

What the visitor has trouble understanding about his friend or relative in rural areas is that the country man likes it here. He likes the calmer pace of life. He likes the cleaner environment. He likes the fact that he needn't fear.

Most importantly, I think, he likes things natural, not man-made. He prefers being in closer touch with the wind and the rain and the sunlight. He values the chance to watch deer browse, to glimpse an occasional eagle or bear, to witness firsthand the cycle of life. He is moved by things the city dweller may never notice; things that have no monetary value but which satisfy his soul. He believes that life today is unnecessarily and unfortunately complex, artificial, and basically silly. And he is sufficiently at peace with himself to be alone from time to time.

But what does he *do*? He does a lot of things.

He appreciates. He ponders. He contemplates. He laughs. He works and reads and helps his neighbors. He gets angry, especially when viewing the evening news. He makes love and plants trees and cuts grass and tries to balance his checkbook. He goes fishing.

He is glad.

Fixing Up

The English word "fix" has an amazing range of meanings. Derived from the Middle English *fixen*, which in turn derives from the Latin *fixus*, it originally meant "to fasten."

Over the years, it has been stretched to include all sorts of notions: to make firm or stable; to preserve for microscopic study; to make a film image permanent; to adjust; to prepare; to mend; to spay or castrate; to get even with; to illegally or improperly influence; to get set.

In the form of a noun, we use "fix" to indicate a predicament, the position of a ship or other craft vis-à-vis the stars, an act of obtaining special privilege or immunity from the law, even the shot of a narcotic.

But the sort of fix I like best has to do with repair or restoration—as in "fix up."

And autumn is the premiere season for fixing up. In spring you do a certain amount of fixing, but it's generally more cleanup than repair. In summer you're too busy living to bother with such truck.

In winter, except for some indoor things, the weather stops you cold.

But come September I find myself busily making lists of things that need fixing. Maybe it's the first frost that triggers this impulse; something to do with battening down for the snowstorms that lie ahead. Or maybe it's just that lots of things suddenly become visible as the leaves fall and the brush thins and the influx of visitors slows. The windowsill that needs paint; the rip in the screen door where the raccoon came visiting; the crack in the sidewalk that could use a bit of patching.

Whatever the reason, I find myself itching to get at this business of fixing up. Out come the paint scraper and the wire brush, the staple gun and the pieces of screen molding I saved from the last time around. One task leads to another; the list of undone jobs grows longer, complete with notes about needed tools and materials. True, the afternoon sun sometimes boils away my ambition and sends me inside for an unplanned nap. But even asleep, I'm apt to dream about fixing. And in the dreams, each project turns out perfectly.

Ah, sweet fixing.

From what secret wellspring does this impulse come? Do we unconsciously yearn to mend a broken, fallen world? Is this urge to fix things somehow connected with dreams of regaining access to a long-lost Eden? Could the desire to mend a torn shirt or sharpen a dull blade or replace a piece of rotted wood be somehow linked to a large, more cosmic urge, uniting us in cocreation with a Higher Power?

I lay no claim to understanding the subterranean source of these desires. But I know beyond doubt that few things are more fulfilling than the act of restoring something damaged to a state of like-new condition.

There's nothing like fixing up—not even a nap.

Narrative

In the meantime, the kids were growing up. We spent the Labor Day weekend of 1987 helping our firstborn, Chris, go off to vocational school in Duluth, to learn the finer points of forest harvesting, including the use of heavy equipment. We shared his excitement at starting a new adventure, but underneath the joy there was the sadness of his absence. For most of our married life, he'd been here with us, as much a part of us as our hands or our hearts, and then, *poof!* He was gone.

We knew, of course, that letting go is what parenting is all about. The entire object of rearing young ones is to prepare them for living on their own. It seems paradoxical that those nights spent anxiously nursing a child through chickenpox or the mumps or a bout with the flu should someday result in saying goodbye, but that is in fact the proper outcome. As any good counselor will tell you, more harm is done by hanging on to your kids than by letting them go. When, a couple years later, our daughter, Kia, went off to college at UMD, we took it in stride, since Chris had led the way.

You Can't Learn Less

M iracles are where you find them.

More accurately, they're forever being overlooked by eyes too world-weary to perceive them. When on occasion we wake up enough to really see into the ordinary things going on around us, *voilà!* We see a miracle.

Take, for example, the thing we call growth. We take for granted that a newborn child will eventually learn to crawl and then to walk and then to talk. But here before us, unfolding with deceptive ease, is a mind-boggling miracle.

Just think of the power inherent in growth. Think of the grandeur. You and I, mere mortals that we are, have within us the capability of improvement in any direction we choose. Barring a specific disability, we can learn to do most anything we want to, assuming we want to badly enough.

We can learn to make music. We can learn to speak French. We can learn to dance, to cast a fly rod, to bake cookies, to fly a plane. If we truly put our minds to it, we could even learn to get organized or to be patient or to remember the name of the person we were introduced to five minutes ago.

The main limits to our growth are the ones we impose upon ourselves. The most common, and the most difficult to overcome, is the assumption that "I could never do that." Often these assumptions are inherited from parents or friends or teachers. Because others expect little from us, we begin to expect little from ourselves. We get mired down into habits of mind, stuck with the same old company, afraid to try anything new.

But life calls to us, to each of us, urging us to grow. The very process of life is growth; the definition of death is no more growth. When we see this clearly, we can better understand why we are instinctively attracted to those folks whose horizons are forever expanding, caught up as they are by the excitement of constant learning. They've grasped the fundamental truth that each newborn so effortlessly displays: life is growth.

The late Buckminster Fuller was such a person. Inventor of the geodesic dome, the Dymaxion car, and dozens of energy-saving devices, in his latter years Fuller became a favorite speaker on college campuses throughout the world. His bubbling style and forward-thinking ideas inspired thousands of young learners.

Above all, Bucky Fuller was an optimist. When asked why he persisted in being so, despite many setbacks and moments of soul-wrenching tragedy, he said he felt he really had no choice, for the simple reason that you can't learn less.

Old Friends

Lately a number of old friends have taken the time to come visit us here in the woods. Some have stopped by for an afternoon's talk, some to stay the night, a few to be with us for several days.

Perhaps it's just coincidence that so many faces from the past have reappeared, but I think not. Instead I suspect it has something to do with the passing of years, some vaguely understood need to measure and compare the progress of one's life with others. As we crest the hill of life and begin our descent toward old age and eventual death, we instinctively seek reassurance and find ourselves looking back, wanting to see and to touch and to find solace in the company of companions from the past.

Whatever the reason, the visits have been fun. Old friends are like walking time machines, able in an instant to transport us into yesteryear. The mere utterance of a name can fling us back, intact, to an experience we thought was forgotten but which in fact is graven vividly in memory.

"Remember when you split your shorts in gym class?" Suddenly the memory of the event rushes up into consciousness and you find yourself, fifty years after the fact, blushing like crazy.

"Remember the day President Kennedy was shot?" Again, the details well up in your brain and you relive those moments of bleak November despair.

Old friends are like extra memory banks, amplifying and augmenting our own ability to recall the past. Because of this, they have a power that newer friends do not. Then, too, they knew us before we became rich or self-righteous or overweight or disillusioned. Knowing this, we find it all but impossible to misrepresent ourselves to them. They are like consciences, demanding accuracy and truth.

But they are also sharers and rememberers of triumphs, comforting and uplifting us by the knowledge they have of our best moments. And because they "go back" with us, they are apt to remind us of earlier aspirations and dreams.

"Did you ever finish that book you were going to write?"

"So how about it—are you still planning to boat down the Mississippi to New Orleans?"

"Whatever happened to the idea you had about trying to grow most of your own food?"

"Did you ever learn to play the ukulele?"

Old friends are comfortable. Having long ago accepted us for who we are, they make few demands upon us. Knowing they'll be there in the pinch helps, too. There is a certain kind of trust that grows up through the years which brings us a vast comfort.

It's true, of course, that too much comfort can be dangerous. If we confine ourselves only to the tried and true, we risk growing stagnant, unchallenged. The very easiness we share can devolve into boredom or stupor. Because old friends are willing to accept our blind spots, they can encourage us to grow overly fond of our biases and preconceptions.

But taken overall, I think there is nothing in the world more valuable than friendships which have weathered the abrasion and pummeling of time. From the random ore of a lifetime's acquaintances, they are our nuggets of gold, worthy at any cost of our safekeeping.

Pillow Talk

Thomas Edison did it. So did Benjamin Franklin. Winston Churchill considered it as important as a good cigar. Lyndon Johnson never let a day go by without indulging in it.

To each of these men, and millions of other men and women world around, taking a daily nap was as vital as eating. To them, life without napping would have seemed stale as an old potato chip, fizzless as leftover champagne.

For as any serious napper knows, daily communion with the pillow is what puts the zing back into one's dulling mind and the little-kid grin back onto one's face. Take away the pillow, and we nappers would probably throw in the towel.

(Actually, that's not quite true. I can recall whole truckloads of GI's fast asleep on the steel floor of a jouncing deuce-and-a-half truck, heads propped on helmets, rifles held lovingly to their chests. Strictly speaking, a pillow isn't necessary, assuming one's fatigue level is in the red zone.)

But under normal conditions, a pillow does help. So does a comfortable bed, couch, air mattress, beach, hammock, recliner, or haystack. Depending on the season, a nice soft blanket adds to the experience, as does the soughing of the wind or the gentle patter of raindrops on the roof. What does not help is the barking of the neighbor's dog, the snarl of a lawn mower, or the insistent jangle of the telephone.

Fortunately, the veteran napper knows these things, and takes care to arrange his life so that dissonant disturbances are avoided. And, if all else fails, he knows just how to wrap the pillow around his head like a giant earmuff.

Once in one's favorite napping vehicle, the next step is the screening out of all practical worries and the commencement of certain special napping thoughts. These can take many forms, ranging from smile-inducing memories of youth to gentle recollections of lapping waves and swaying palms to visions of astral voyage. The important thing is that the thoughts are essentially soothing in nature. No place here for anything strenuous or strident. The trick is to lower, not raise, the pulse rate; a grown-up version of after-school cookies and milk.

Finally, the napper attends to attaining his or her favorite posture. This can take a while, but the effort is justified. By positioning the legs with just the right amount of knee-flex, scrunching the arms into a comfy, self-cradling curve, and making the necessary adjustments of cranium to pillow, the napper is ready to drop off.

A yawn or two, a sigh, one final wiggle of the head, and the napper begins the delicious descent beneath the waves of conscious thought, down-down-down into the blissful depths of sleep, knowing as he sinks that he will slip, in his final flicker of awareness, beyond the grip of all worries and cares.

The Phoebes

Saturday, 7 a.m. I sit in the screen porch, sipping coffee and marveling at the sounds that fill the spring air.

From the lake come the insistent honk of geese, the quack of mallards, the trill of red-winged blackbirds, the manic yodel of loons.

From the woods I hear the liquid melody of robins, the sad lament of mourning doves, the cheerful riff of chickadees, and the raucous proclamations of a band of crows.

A month ago this part of the world lay white and silent, shrouded by snow. Now it buzzes and bustles with reemergent life, many forms of which have wings. Like their counterparts the tourists, some of these visitors will linger temporarily before moving on to other destinations. Most of the geese will fly further north before setting up their summer camps. The sandhill cranes and trumpeter swans that graced our lake the week before are probably already in Canada. For them and for dozens of other waterfowl species, this place we call home is only a flyover zone.

I go back into the house for a refill of coffee. When I return, I see a songbird perched on a birch branch, silent but by no means still. At frequent intervals its tail flicks down and up, down and up, like a third-base coach flashing a sign. Aha! Ms. Phoebe (or maybe Mr.), come back to raise another brood of kids.

For the dozens of years we've occupied this particular piece of land, phoebes have spent the summers with us, civilizing our homestead with their unobtrusive ways. They are wary and shy, like most of their wild counterparts, but not so much as to be scared away by humans.

Each year for decades, members of their clan have chosen to build their nurseries under the protective overhangs of our buildings. Some years we've counted as many as six separate nests; out by the chicken coop, down by the shop, on the north wall of the house, at various locations around the garage. This year, it appears, will be no exception.

I settle in to watch as Ms. Phoebe begins setting up house. I'm reasonably sure it's a she, because I've spied a second bird perched a dozen feet away who follows her activities with careful interest and begins assisting in the job at hand, as befits a first mate. In the world of birds, it's generally Mama who rules the roost, so chances are this helper is male and, now that the business of procreation has been attended to, will play a supporting role in the coming domestic drama.

According to phoebe protocol, the first step after mating is homebuilding. I watch as Mama glides down to the edge of our terrace and pulls a tuft of moss from its place on the stone wall. Phoebes make nests of weeds, grasses, fibers, and mud, like many other songbirds, but they go a step further and cover their work with moss before lining it with fine grasses and hair. The nests are built mostly by females, and take anywhere from a couple of days to a couple of weeks for completion. I wait till Mama's added the moss to her construction, then amble down to the garage to take a peek. Sure enough, the nest is well along, a semicircular work sitting atop the board I nailed under the eaves years ago, fastened tight to the adjacent rafter and safely protected from rain.

By Sunday evening the nest is nearly finished. As near as I can tell, both Mama and mate have worked nonstop all weekend long, preparing a safe nursery for the offspring-to-come. They watch from a distance as I inspect their work, but make no comment when I say, "Well done."

I wish I could tell them more, wish that our languages weren't so dissimilar. If I could, I would tell them how proud I am of their excellent work, and praise them for the dedication they'll exhibit in the weeks ahead, carefully incubating the eggs Mama will lay in the nest, and then tending for endless hours to the hungry demands of their young brood.

Like most other wild things, this little pair of parents will devote themselves completely to the job of raising their kids; a diligence that puts some human parenting to shame.

Blind Spots

I f you've driven a car you know all about blind spots, those places where you just can't see what's happening. You get ready to pull into the passing lane, check your mirrors, put on your turn signal, and start to shift lanes when—HONK, the driver behind you lets you know you almost drove him off the road.

Blind spots are scary. You back down the driveway and find you've crushed an unseen bike, and realize with thumping heart that instead it could have been a child. You start through a crosswalk and stop just in time to avoid turning an oncoming pedestrian—hidden from view by your windshield post—into a hood ornament. You prepare to turn onto a busy highway, hear the sudden screech of brakes, and mutter to your passengers that you "just didn't see him coming."

Blind spots extend beyond streets and highways.

If you see one of the political parties as peopled primarily with crooks and low-life scum while the other appears blameless, you've probably got a blind spot. If you're certain America (or your church or school or family) can do no wrong, you've probably got another one. If you're the only person you know who's consistently right about everything, you've got a major one.

It's impossible, of course, for any of us to see all things accurately. Being human means being imperfect, and being imperfect implies having blind spots. But some are worse than others. As any member of a twelve-step group will attest, self-deception can hide many a dysfunction from view, including some monstrous ones. Nor does it help when the society at large encourages turning a blind eye to things like substance abuse, spouse or child beating, addictive gambling, or other forms of harmful activity.

Regarding certain items, we almost seem united in denial. Take nuclear waste. (Wouldn't it be wonderful if someone *could*?) While we argue vehemently among ourselves over the issue of abortion, we seem curiously tolerant of the growing mountain of radioactive material capable of turning millions of fetuses into misshapen mutants, and causing unspeakable grief for anyone else exposed to its toxic rays.

Or take ordinary, consumer-variety, waste. We generate it at a rate far higher than any other group of people anywhere. And what do we do with it? In the main, we bury it. Where? In the ground, on top of our water supply. Why? So we don't have to see it or smell it. Out of sight, out of mind. A national blind spot, and one which, like the proverbial skeleton in the closet, is someday sure to haunt us.

Few things are more painful than having our blind spots revealed. By nature we think of ourselves as competent, decent, and reasonable. It's the other guy whose qualities we question. But part of true maturity is learning to see ourselves as objectively as possible, to admit our shortcomings and misconceptions, and to work at correcting them.

How do we find them? Start with the things we're most certain about. Certainty masks distortion.

Why bother? St. Augustine, a man of many passions with a fierce regard for truth, summed it thus: "This is the very perfection of a man, to find out his own imperfections."

Different Stories

O ne of the least-noticed facts about us humans is that we learn who we are through stories. Stories explain how we fit into the larger social patterns and provide us with blueprints for building a conscience. Unlike other animals, we are language-dependent. Take away words and we're reduced to the level of the higher primates: close, but not quite human.

To be sure, much of what defines us is nonlingual. Starting before birth, nestled in the womb, an unborn child absorbs all sorts of information about the world in which he or she will be living. Temperature, mood, the beat of mother's heart, the rhythms of day and night—these and hundreds of other clues are gradually revealed well in advance of actual launching.

Then, in a rite of passage equaled in importance only by eventual death, the child is delivered into the world and the process of sorting things out intensifies. *Is it safe out here in the open air? Ah, here comes a blanket. That's better. Is Mom OK? Whew! She's stopped screaming and started making cooing sounds. Am I gonna get fed? Oh, good, here comes the milk.*

Each of these events helps us understand who we are. Newborns who are not held and cuddled conclude, quite logically, that they must not be very important—an opinion that will govern their actions for a lifetime. Infants subjected to parental stress are apt to be high-strung themselves. Diet, hygiene, protection from danger, prompt attention to bodily needs—all these and more go into forming who we are and how we think of ourselves.

In addition, we carry within ourselves certain genetic proclivities which we can never escape. A propensity toward laughter or melancholy, toward sickness or robust health, the color of our hair and eyes, even traits such as shyness or chumminess are all determined largely by the gene pool out of which we swim.

We are products of nature, yes. But we are deeply shaped by nurture. And the primary tool of nurture is the telling of stories.

Think back to your earliest years, and chances are you remember someone telling you stories. Whether read from a book or spoken from memory, stories are ways of interpreting the world, of fitting things together so they make sense.

Cultural differences are essentially based on different stories. Notions of marriage and kinship, status and social role, property and politics—all grow out of shared tales. Even our perception of skin color is largely determined by the stories we've heard. In one Native American creation tale, the Great Spirit fashions the first man from clay, puts him in the oven to give him life, leaves him too long, and is dismayed to find him charred and overdone. On the second attempt, the little man comes out pasty white and undercooked. But on the third try the Creator gets it right, and the man comes out copper-skinned and perfect.

To a young child hearing this story, it becomes self-evident that only people with copper skin are normal, and that those with lighter or darker shades are somehow flawed.

If, at our mother's knee, we learn that God loves Christians but not Jews or Muslims or Buddhists or agnostics, we will think and act in ways far different from someone who learned that the Creator exhorts us to have compassion for other sentient beings and to consider them all our brothers and sisters.

Once a year we take to heart the words of the angel in the story of Jesus's birth and fervently wish one another peace on earth. But there can be no peace until we begin to see beyond our own specific stories, and to embrace those whose stories differ from ours.

Peace will come when, and only when, we learn to welcome and to celebrate human diversity, and to view all people as valued members of the family of man.

Narrative

Our growing interest in stone led, in time, to the building of a cottage we dubbed the Stonehouse and which we operated as a bed-and-breakfast. We opened it for business in the fall of 1989 and, as it turned out, ran it for almost ten years. During that period our lives were graced and enriched by many new friendships, several of which have continued to the present. Guests slept down in the Stonehouse near the shore of Lund Lake, some 300 feet from our house, but came up to the house for breakfast. It didn't take long for us to realize that Claire's cooking was a major reason folks kept coming back. Fresh eggs from our flock of chickens, crisp produce from the garden, plenty of locally harvested wild rice, and home-baked bread made from freshly ground wheat all acted as culinary magnets. Looking back, some of our finest memories occurred around the breakfast table, with conversations often extending an hour or two beyond mealtime.

One perennial topic of conversation here in the north woods is the weather. The winter of 1991-'92 proved to be quite uncommon, and provoked lots of nervous talk. First we had a terrible blizzard in the end of October—and then everything got warm and abnormal, and we all began to get uptight. "It Ain't Over Yet" delves into the psychology of winter-ready Minnesotans, and how unnerving it is to us when things don't work out badly.

Better, by far, to follow the wisdom inherent in adjusting our thoughts to align with reality. There are dozens of ways to make ourselves crazy: getting angry at the stupidity of others, taking umbrage at a lack of civility and respect, wanting the world to be different than it is, trying to control the folks around us. As the essays in this section indicate, such efforts gain us nothing but more grief. The trick instead is to go with the flow of energy all around us, and learn to use it constructively.

It Ain't Over Yet

O ne of the dizziest delights of living in this part of the world is the Wheel-of-Fortune nature of the climate. As the old adage has it, if you don't like the weather, just wait ten minutes. A summer storm is apt to give way to cloudless skies; a winter blizzard may well be followed by an unseasonable thaw.

The mercurial nature of our climate keeps boredom at bay, and in the process serves to hold us in a properly humble state. Unlike citizens of southern California, say, we Minnesotans can never bank on the fact that tomorrow will be just like today.

Generally, this uncertainty helps to make us cheerful people. Having seen how often the tables turn, we learn to endure the disagreeable, knowing that it will soon pass and be replaced by something more to our liking. Where others might see life-threatening terror, we see humor: 40 below keeps the riffraff away. We put our pests on pedestals (the mosquito as state bird) and hoot at our horrors through bumper-sticker art ("Snow happens").

But the one situation we can't handle is when things get too good for too long, as has been the case with this winter of 1991-'92. Mild temps, manageable snowfalls, an uncommon number of snow-graced and hoar-frosted picture-book landscapes; events such as these conspire to bring our paranoia out of the closet and onto Main Street.

Braced to expect the worst, we grow weak and confused in the face of the best. The very qualities that serve us so well in normal, nose-freezing winters (our stoicism and "whatever" pessimism) sour in the unaccustomed heat and turn ugly.

All winter long, except for that freak October storm, we've been waiting dutifully for grief to assail us. We expect it; that's what happens in winter; we want it.

Yes, want it. You can't live up here year after year without nurturing some perverse delight in pain. We're northerners, for pity's sake. We're winter-hardy people. We can take it. Give us your best shot!

When it doesn't happen, when for one magic winter the abuse is held in abeyance and we can actually go outside and enjoy it, we turn contrary and stay inside, confused.

Listen to the talk around you. Hear the guarded optimism of those who predict a butt-kicking blizzard in March. See the dour faces all around you, the faces craving pain.

What kind of winter is this? It's almost embarrassing, that's what it is. A jet-stream joke, stratospheric patterns gone amok.

But it ain't over yet. We mustn't give up hope.

There's still time for the hammer to fall.

Road Game

A recent trip to attend a wedding in northern Illinois got me thinking about an antidote to road rage. Like everyone else, I've occasionally gotten a trifle heated at the insanity/incompetence/impatience of my fellow drivers; but this trip made two things exceedingly clear.

One: the number of idiots on the road is increasing daily.

Two: unless you want to experience the questionable thrill of having an apoplectic fit, you better learn how to laugh.

Let me enlarge upon point two. What difference does it make if the guy behind you suddenly decides to pass just as on oncoming car tops the hill ahead of you? Odds are you'll either survive the near miss, or you'll be dead on impact. Either way, you can't do much about it, so why not chill out and enjoy the ride?

How? For starters, try identifying the various types of madness around you, the way you would birds or wildflowers. Think of it as a variant of the "I spy with my little eye" game you played as a kid.

For example, the fellow who, on a four-lane divided highway, insists on driving in the left lane. Call him Lefty. Lefty's a law-abiding dude who sets his cruise control precisely at the posted speed limit. He might start out in the right lane, where he belongs, but sooner or later he comes up on someone driving slower than himself and shifts to the left lane to pass. Once in that lane, he stays there, usually for 20 or 30 miles, chatting amiably to his passengers and feeling righteous as an altar boy. No matter that his mindlessness raises the blood pressure of everyone behind him, interrupting the flow of things like a blood clot in an artery. He's obeying the speed limit, so everything's cool.

Or take the gal who, on a two-lane road, passes left-turning cars on the right. Call her Righty. Unable to bear the thought of losing precious seconds waiting for the guy in front to complete his turn, Righty rams around him on the shoulder, oblivious to the possibility of bikers or pedestrians dead ahead, not caring whether the shoulder is even paved. Except in designated turnouts this is an illegal act, but Righty could care less. All she knows is that she's in a hurry, and left-turning traffic is a bother and a bore, easily ignored by zipping around on the right.

Another fun driver, related to Righty by an obsessive need to keep moving, is one we might call Mister Passer. Mister Passer is usually young and exhibits a fascinating lack of judgment, especially when it comes to gauging distance. Clearly driven by a desire to live life on the edge, Mister Passer can't stand being behind another vehicle, and solves his problem by compulsive passing. He does not execute his moves with grace. Instead he roars up to your rear bumper, rides behind you like a NASCAR driver grabbing draft, waits for an oncoming semi, and then hammers the accelerator in a death-defying bid to get around you before smashing head-on into the approaching truck. He does this again and again, jerking in and out of his appointed lane like a high-strung jockey on amphetamines.

When you get to the next stoplight you find he's gained exactly one car length.

Or take MP's mirror image, PM. Putz Meister's a laid-back creature, prefers two-lane roads, and is out to enjoy the journey. To do so he deducts 15 miles from the posted limit and stays at that. Like Lefty on the four-lane, Putz Meister revels in the warmth of self-righteousness. Not for him the rampant impatience of Righty or Mister Passer. PM's a country kind of guy, checking out the pretty trees, the grazing cows, the lone crow pecking at road kill. Like Mister Magoo, he's blessedly unaware of the clenched bowels and frantic maneuvers he provokes in other drivers, and would vigorously deny causing a jumble of mishaps behind him.

The creative reader can add to this list and take the Road Game to greater delights. But at least you have a starting point, and a way to alchemize the bile of road rage into the milk and honey of good humor.

Life's too precious to allow your underwear to knot up. Next time you're out driving, play the game. And laugh.

Sticks, Stones, and Words

According to the old children's ditty, "Sticks and stones may break my bones, but words can never hurt me."

Maybe not physically. But words have a way of lingering in the memory, especially when they're unkind. And unkind words are a form of violence. They jar the serenity of the person at whom they're aimed. They diminish self-confidence. And they definitely provoke feelings of aggression.

Everybody knows this. Yet the tide of verbal violence seems to swell by the day, cheered on by talk-show hosts and rappers, with plenty of reinforcement in other forms of popular entertainment such as satellite radio and mainstream movies.

As teachers will tell you, the kind of language once confined to the locker room has moved into the hallway and on into the classroom, where today it has come to seem almost normal. A variety of four-letter words trip heartily from the lips of students barely out of kindergarten, disrupting concentration, undermining all sense of authority, and generally wreaking academic havoc.

What are teachers to do?

I know what Mr. Witte did.

Mr. Witte was my freshman science teacher in high school. He was brand-new to our school, and hence some students felt the need to test him. Matter of fact, the guy I shared a lab table with, named Butch, was the first to probe Mr. Witte's tolerance level by muttering the infamous "f-word" just loud enough for Witte to hear. An instant later Herr Witte came bounding over the intervening tables, grabbed Butch by the seat of his jeans and the back of his neck, hoisted him into the air, and carried him bodily out into the hallway, where he proceeded to grind him against the cinderblock wall as he stomped toward the principal's office.

While he was gone, the rest of us sat quietly, contemplating the fact that further testing of the man might be unwise. Did we feel terrified? Not at all. I think most of us felt quite relieved, because we knew that Butch was in the wrong and Witte was in the right and justice, however primitive, had been done.

Today, of course, a teacher's hands are virtually tied by a well-intentioned and absolutely asinine cluster of laws forbidding physical "violence" except in self-defense. As a consequence, students are allowed to practice verbal violence without fear of recrimination, thereby further eroding the authority that all young people vitally need.

If kids can't respect adults, how can they grow to respect themselves? We all learn by imitating. We imitate words, we imitate actions, and we certainly imitate attitudes.

What many adults are saying to kids today is that anything goes, and that nothing (except, perhaps, money) is worthy of their respect. Kids, being the perceptive critters they are, respond by pushing things to the limit—only to find that the limit constantly evades them, surrendered by adults who are either too frightened or too apathetic to hold the line.

Sticks and stones may indeed break our bones. But it's also true that words, used as instruments of disrespect, can do us all a great deal of damage.

Third-Person Therapy

Language is a tricky thing.

Absorbing it as we do in infancy, we tend not to think much about it except when misunderstandings arise. Most of the time we speak with the same ease that we breathe.

What goes unnoticed is that language conditions the way we think. Some linguists insist that thought itself is not possible without language. Imagine yourself thinking about getting a drink of water, and then try to imagine the same thought without the words "drink" or "water," and you'll see what they mean.

Because English has past, present, and future tenses, we automatically sort events into those categories, and think of something that happened yesterday or last year as fixed in time, telling ourselves, "what's done is done." But several Native American languages have no past tense; their speakers think of earlier events as ongoing into the future.

Furthermore, we divide the world into three additional parts in order to make it correspond to what English teachers call "point of view" or "person." In first person, when speaking of an individual, we say "I"; in second, "you," and in third, "he, she, or it." When speaking of more than one person, we use the words "we," "you," and "they."

This convention has some profound outcomes. For one thing, it sets up divisions among us of which we are generally unaware. The late newspaper columnist Sydney Harris made it a lifelong habit to bring these divisions to his readers' attention with statements such as the following: "I'm a man of firm principles, you tend to be stubborn, he's pigheaded"; "I read relaxing books, you read escape fiction, he reads trash"; and "I have an appreciative eye for the ladies, you're an incurable flirt, he's an old lecher."

The power with which the language molds us is impossible to overestimate, simply because it's so hard to see. We take for granted, as if it were a force like gravity or a fixture such as the North Star, that "I" matters more than "you" or "he." This artificial division plays right into the hands of our reigning economic system, capitalism, with its mythology of rugged individualism and a dog-eat-dog world. But life, to be truly satisfying, must include cooperation as well as competition. Poll after poll of the American people indicates a deep-seated hunger for greater community, a cry for spiritual sustenance different from the rewards of mere financial gain.

In order for this to happen, we need to think inclusively rather than exclusively, to stress our similarities rather than our differences. A good first step is to work at seeing ourselves as objectively as possible. And a simple way to do this lies readily at hand.

All we need to do is start thinking of ourselves in the third person, singular: he or she instead of I.

If we step, as it were, outside of ourselves, and imagine ourselves observing ourselves, magical things happen. Instead of being tied like infants to the dictates of our egos, unaware of our impact on those around us, we can learn to see ourselves as others might see us.

It could even be fun to pretend we are novelists, and jot down a few lines of third-person description: "He woke a half-hour late, snarled at his wife on the way out the door, drove like a maniac to work, and spent the day being sullen and crabby to all those around him." Or "She smiled at the indecisive customer and patiently answered all his questions, knowing what it was like to be on the other side of the counter." Or "At first he felt irritated that Jenks had won the trophy; but when he remembered the surge of pride he himself had felt upon winning it last year, he clapped Jenks on the shoulder and said, 'I'm really happy for you.'"

Try it. There's little to lose, other than an over-inflated sense of our own self-importance. And losing some of that might just improve our lives.

The Keys

I t happens every year, just before Christmas. Having put off the search for gifts until the number of remaining shopping days dips into the single digits, I find myself standing in line surrounded by hundreds of fellow procrastinators. Tinny Yuletide music bleats forth from the store's loudspeakers. The temperature hovers around 90. Trapped in winter clothing, insulated boots awash with sweat, I clutch the handle of the shopping cart like a castaway clinging to flotsam.

Excellent, whimpers my fevered brain. *Way to go. Way to plan. Way to suffer. Next year why don't you wait till Christmas Eve to start your shopping?*

I try to ignore these sour-grapes murmurs by concentrating on the crush of people around me. Ahead I see a tall gaunt fellow staring ceilingward as if in prayer. To the side a plump lady backhands a youngster trying to peek in a bag. Behind me a fellow about my own age rocks back and forth, back and forth, eyes closed, as if on the verge of mental breakdown.

My brain continues to complain. *So this is Christmas, eh pal? This is what it's really all about? Standing in line to spend your money, waiting like a sheep to be shorn? Shuffling down the aisle picking baubles*

150

from the racks like some poor primitive preparing to trade his homeland for a few glass beads?

The line moves forward several millimeters. A gaggle of giggling teen girls wriggles crosswise through the gridlocked lines. No mental problems here. I watch their laughing faces, try to count the number of earrings they collectively wear, watch as they disappear into the herd.

Then I see him. A stocky dude with brush-cut hair wearing a black leather jacket and a look of smoldering rebellion, like some character in an early Marlon Brando film. He stands there glowering like a volcano working up steam. He has no shopping cart, for his purchases are only two: a box of chocolates and a little bottle of perfume.

Seeing this, I cannot help but smile. Our eyes meet and to my great surprise Mr. Rebel smiles back!

I look around, look all around, see with fresh eyes the dozens of people inching forward with their gifts, and realize with amazing clarity that this ritual is not about money, not about things, not about obligation.

This Christmas thing, this money-guzzling, bone-fatiguing, mind-frying game we play each year is still, and always will be, about love.

The Christ child may get lost behind the tinsel and the ribbons, but not for long. His face is visible everywhere, each time someone gives and someone cares. And timeworn as it might be, the urge to celebrate His birthday is one of our finest and most commendable longings: the yearning to transcend our private concerns and open our hearts to one another.

Once open, we are as vulnerable as a baby lying on a straw pile, and as filled with power as the universe is vast.

And the gifts? I saw most unmistakably that they are the keys we use to unlock not the other's heart, but our own.

Letting Go

Fresh out of New Year's resolutions?

How about adopting mine?

This year I resolve to let go of everything that bogs me down. Every possession, every memento, every relationship, every fantasy, every preoccupation with the past—everything that blocks my growth and saps my ability to revel in the gift of life: all of these things I propose to throw overboard.

I intend to enrich my life by simplifying it. Not by avoiding legitimate responsibilities or by shirking hard work, but by being honest about what does and does not bring me happiness.

My books, for example. I'm a compulsive collector of books. Always have been. And I never seem able to part with a book once I've got it, even if it's garbage. I have books in such pitiful condition a librarian would retch. Books all over the place, spilling off overcrowded coffee tables and bulging out of cartons and preempting shelf space that should go to useful items such as towels and canned goods and toilet paper.

The obvious thing is to get rid of some of them. Clean house. Prune back the excess branches so that new life has room for growth.

It's the same with habits and relationships and security blankets. Many of these start out by bringing us joy. But over the years they begin to encrust us, keeping us from growth. As the years go by and we find ourselves increasingly encumbered, it's easy to forget that life is a process, that to live often means to outlive, that to grow is to outgrow and let go.

Nature abounds with examples of this process. The lobster, for instance, can grow only if it sheds a series of hard, protective shells. The carapace that served it well at one stage eventually becomes too small for its enlarging body. If the shell cannot be dropped as the lobster expands, it will smother and gradually kill its owner. But letting go of the shell is also a risk. When the protective cover is gone the lobster is left soft, pliable, and vulnerable to attack. It's only in this unguarded state that it can create a new and expanded covering that allows for continued growth.

The mandate of life is change. As the philosopher Henri Bergson insisted, life is flux. If we fail to grow, to change, to let go of the past, in that measure do we forfeit a portion of life.

It isn't the goal that matters so much as the reaching toward it. And to reach well, to work and to love and to live with gusto, the less excess baggage the better.

As the new year begins, take stock. Look around; think; be honest. Then act. All that impedes you, all that oppresses you, all that stifles the life inside you deserves to be changed. If you can throw it away, do so. If you can do without it, do without. Get lean. Uncomplicate things. Make room in your life for the things and the people and the experiences that really count.

Give life a chance. Let go.

Residual Thoughts

Years ago it was the fashion for column writers like myself to salt their work with little gems of wisdom and moral insight. The theory was that the reader needed and could benefit from occasional injections of philosophical go-juice, sort of a Vitamin P to lift the sagging spirits and ward off the infections of wrong thinking.

Nowadays, of course, we pretend to know better. Wisdom, we seem certain, is neither contagious nor communicable. When it comes to earning insight, it's every person for him—or herself.

But the idea of offering gifts to the reader dies hard. What, after all, do we writers of columns have to say? We can pass on some humor and maybe an interesting story now and then, but when you take a truthful inventory, our supply of goodies gets to looking rather sparse.

As the old year waned, I found myself scribbling little messages on Post-It Notes and sticking the notes in prominent places lest they fall into the heap on my desk and be lost for decades. Taken together, these notes would comprise a New Year's gift to my beloved readers; sort of a Whitman's Sampler of yummy mental bonbons.

Then I thought of Forrest Gump and his famous admonition about life being like a box of chocolates, and the whole concept suddenly seemed comical.

After much head scratching and some despair, I decided instead to offer what might best be called residual thoughts—the stuff that's left after the frivolities have boiled away. Here they are.

Work Hard. Work has a tonic effect upon the spirit. Hard work unites you with others, including those who have gone before. Hard work allows little room for self-pity, excuses, idle gossip, or untruth. Honest work has a valuable side product: dignity.

Don't Be Afraid. Fear corrupts. It comes from inside yourself, not from outside. You can control it by stating what it is you fear and why. Most of the time fear is based on "ifs." Take one step at a time and let the "ifs" be damned.

Try to Understand Things. Much of the world's confusion comes from individuals not taking the time to try to understand themselves and others. It's hard to love or even tolerate that which you don't understand. Bigotry, intolerance, insensitivity, being set in your ways—all indicate weakness, not strength. We are born with the capacity to understand just about anything. All we have to do is try.

Try Not to Hurt Anyone. Not a popular idea in recent decades, but an ancient and noble goal. Life is short. Why inflict unnecessary pain? Whenever we damage someone else, we also do damage to ourselves, resulting in guilt, hardness of heart, and a diminished capacity to love. The bully is always insecure. It takes strength and a clear-eyed acceptance of yourself not to be bossy, offensive, blind to the needs and sufferings of others. Not one of us has the right to wreak harm.

Stay Calm. Things rarely work out as well or as poorly as we think they will. A calm and steady heart contributes to the cosmic joy.

Narrative

As readers familiar with an earlier book, *A Place Called Home*, will know, Claire and I lost our only daughter to the ravages of ovarian cancer on June 19, 1998. At the time of her death, Kia was 26 and a high school art teacher at St. Peter, MN, in love with her work and her husband, Rick, and beloved by her students and colleagues.

In the aftermath of Kia's death, we had no choice but to close the Stonehouse as a B&B. Since we served breakfast up at our house, and since, except on weekends, I had to go off to work every morning, Claire was left to entertain guests while simultaneously trying to cook meals from scratch and deal with the loss of her daughter, who also happened to be her best friend. The situation was untenable. At the end of the year we closed the Stonehouse to guests and began renting it out as a year-around house.

When classes resumed in the fall, St. Peter High School commemorated Kia with the release of hundreds of butterflies, and Claire and I began the habit of lighting a memorial candle in her honor each night at suppertime, which we continue doing to this day.

Like others before us who have lost a child, we've come to understand that you never "get over" the pain and heartache, and in fact you wouldn't want to, since that's one of the ways you stay connected to the loved one you lost. Instead you try to focus on the hundreds of happy memories that preceded the agony of loss, and honor the beloved's memory in every way you can.

For us it's taken the form of telling our grandchildren all about their Auntie Kia; of visiting her grave and tending to her monument; of displaying some of her many paintings and sculptures in our house and giving others to her friends and loved ones; of awarding a scholarship in her memory every spring to a deserving graduate of our local high school; of helping to raise awareness about the symptoms and nature of ovarian cancer and the importance of early detection; and of talking openly and without reservation about the feelings of joy and sorrow that we continue to have toward her.

Beyond that we can do little, and as the years have passed since her death, we're learning to cut ourselves loose from mistaken feelings of obligation and emotional debt. Our sweet princess is gone. We hope someday to be reunited with her, and with the many other loved ones who have passed away, but we don't presume to know if this will happen. In the meantime we cherish and celebrate the loved ones who remain part of our lives; our son, Chris, and our daughter-in-law, Sara; our grandchildren, Levi and Grace and Jack; our many relatives and friends; and the hundreds of artists and writers and musicians who continue to grace our lives through their creations.

It is my firm conviction that being alive is a gift of immeasurable value. The best way to honor that gift is to live life as cleanly and well as you can. One of the most effective ways to do that is by spending time with the people you love. It sounds—and is—quite obvious, but many of us manage to botch the job, and often fail to put our resources where our hearts are.

Five Guys

F ather's Day dawns clear and cool. I shower, shave, and take a cup of fresh-brewed coffee out to the screen porch, to greet the day and to remember.

A robin works its way across the yard in search of worms with which to feed its young. The little ones are perched high above the ground in a nest the mother built a month ago, and they're insatiable. Like babies everywhere, they expect to be fed whenever they're hungry—and they're hungry all the time.

Lesson One: In most species, after impregnating Mother, Father's primary duty is to provide food. Whether the nourishment comes from a hole in the ground or the shelf of a supermarket, the kids need to eat.

I close my eyes and see my long-dead grandfather at the summer cottage poking holes in the garden soil with his index finger. "Put the seeds in there," he says. "One in each hole." I squat down and follow his instructions, pulling the pea seeds, one at a time, from the packet and dropping them into the holes. When I'm finished, Grandpa smoothes the dirt with the back of his rake and impales the empty packet on a stick to mark the row. "Good job," he says, as we stand to admire our work. He puts his big hand on my shoulder. "Now

let's go fill your sprinkling can so you can give them some water."
We walk to the hand pump at the side of the yard and commence to
fill the can. My dad is gone off to something called a war to fight a
man named Hitler, and can't be here to help. But Gramps says we'll
take pictures when the peas come up, and send them overseas. "He'll
get a kick out of that," says Gramps. "Your daddy'll be real proud
of you."

I open my eyes and stare out at the sunlight pushing through
the trees, then turn to look up at the garden. Not many years ago
my own son delighted in walking through the rows of vegetables,
pulling out a carrot or snapping off a snow-pea for consumption on
the spot. He was still in diapers then, and loved to walk barefoot and
wiggle his toes in the dirt. Now he's got kids of his own, a boy and
a girl, and one of the joys of my life is that my father was able to see
them before he died.

How can the years pass so quickly? What alchemy makes possible
this incredible blurring of time? Last week I went for a walk with my
grandson, Levi, already three-and-a-half. During the walk we talked
about growing things, and he said he was going to plant some peas
in the family garden. I stopped in my tracks, struck dumb by the
fact that things had come full circle.

"What's the matter, Grandpa?"

I shook my head, overcome with emotion.

"Is something wrong?"

It took me a moment to speak. "No," I said, putting my hand on
his shoulder. "Everything's as it should be. Everything's just dandy."

He smiled then, and repeated the phrase "just dandy." The kid
loves words. Come to think of it, so did my dad and my grandpa,

and so does my son, and so do I. Five guys, and every one of them getting a kick out of language.

On the way back to the house Levi broke into a run. "I'll race you, Grandpa," he said, excited. I made a show of competing, but let him pull ahead. Best to enjoy the carefree years and build up a good store of happy memories. Before he knew it he, too, would be a dad, worried about feeding the little ones.

But that's all right, I thought, running faster. Life's a big looping circle, not a straight line. And each of our lives interlink with the generations before and after our own, making us part of an ancient, ongoing chain.

Which strikes me as being just dandy.

Island Time

Like many other winter-weary northerners, my wife and I recently managed to fly south for a week and partake of the glories of tropical living.

Specifically, we went to the Bahamas, to join another couple on a little island off the eastern coast of Greater Abaco called Elbow Cay (pronounced "key"). Elbow Cay is small and skinny, running seven miles from north to south and averaging less than half a mile in width. But what it might lack in size it more than makes up in character. It's a genuine island, reachable only by helicopter or boat, and sports palm trees and hammocks rather than casinos and high-rise hotels.

Like its hundreds of counterparts throughout the Caribbean, Elbow Cay runs on island time. This prompts the need for certain adjustments. "A minute" might mean half an hour; "later" might turn out to be tomorrow; "tomorrow" could stretch into a couple of days or even a week. But that's okay.

Where is it written that strict punctuality confers virtue? Who says timeliness is next to godliness? Who cares?

As a new arrival slathered in sunscreen and ambling down the beach, you begin to suspect that your northerly fixation with schedules and clock time is in fact a habit of questionable value. Here on a speck of land where the next continent to the east is Africa, the idea of subdividing days into hours and minutes and seconds seems silly. The day starts when you get out of bed and ends when you can't drink another Goombay Smash and you wander off to sleep. In between you may require naps, or at the very least some hammock time. Whatever.

Nor do your daily responsibilities much matter. Aside from the core tasks like taking on tasty nourishment and keeping your vitamin C level topped off with various fruit-juice-based drinks, your main assignments involve lolling in the pool or searching the beach for shells, with maybe a dollop of snorkeling for the super ambitious. And life is getting easier with each passing year. Last time we visited Elbow Cay, we were forced to pedal around the island on fat-tired one-speed bikes. Now, with the coming of more civilized ways, we were able to rent a golf cart.

Which is not to indicate that we fell prey to the dangers of tropical lassitude. All members of our party were alert to the importance of self-discipline, and made it a point to present ourselves promptly at each of the day's three mealtimes. In addition, we kept our intellectual skills honed by reading interesting brochures, studying the ingredients listed on the labels of Kalik beer bottles, and discussing the possible whereabouts of buried treasure left behind by the colorful pirates who once inhabited these parts.

All in all, our trip to the Bahamas proved valuable and refreshing, and gave each of us an opportunity to measure our north-country lifestyles against those of more laid-back climes. Now that we've returned, we've stopped listening to MPR and sing along instead with old Jimmy Buffet albums, and have begun planning our return to the islands at some point in the future. The only problem is we've lost interest in looking at calendars, and try as I might (which I think was sometime last week) I can't find my watch.

Smart Shopper

L ast week I decided to buy a laptop computer.

Being a person of thrifty habits, I decided right off that I would take the time necessary to inform myself of the various choices involved. Rather than rush to a retailer and buy the first machine that caught my eye, I would approach things rationally and with a calm skepticism, balancing cost against features in order to determine the best value.

Since I use a computer primarily for word processing, I knew I didn't need anything with an abundance of bells and whistles. "The simpler the better," I told my wife. "Kind of like a Model T car."

"I'm not too sure you'll find that, Honey. But maybe you will. Good luck."

But when I began pawing through the advertising supplements in the Sunday paper, it quickly became clear that no one was marketing a Model T laptop. It also became clear that comparing one model with another was not an apples-to-apples activity.

"256 MB DDR2 memory, 60 GB hard drive, integrated 802.11g wireless LAN, 4-in-1 digital media manager, 14" Ultrabright wide screen, with instant $100 savings, $599.99," said one ad.

"Intel Core Solo Processor T1300 (1.66 GHz), 1 GB Shared Dual-Channel DDR2 SDRAM, 80 GB Hard Drive, CD/DVD burner. 17" Widescreen XGA+ Display," said another. "Pre-Savings cost $1528, now only $1099."

"15.4" BrightView screen, AMD Turion 64 Processor, ML-37 Notebook with LightScribe, DVD-RW Drive, 1024MB DDR Memory, 60 GB Hard Drive," said a third, offering a $20 instant rebate and a $30 mail-in rebate for a total price of $929.99.

I counseled myself to stay calm. This was, after all, not a major purchase like a car or house. Millions of others have managed to find their way through the confusing maze of choices. The trick was to stay objective.

"What word-processing program are you running on your desktop?" asked a clerk at one of the big box stores. He appeared to be at least thirteen, much older than the last clerk I'd talked to.

"Microsoft Word. But the computer itself is a Mac."

"Ah. Then you'll have to buy the software separately if you go with a PC laptop."

"How much is that?"

"It depends. Microsoft has a variety of packages. We might get you set up for around $100. But it could go as high as $350, depending on what you want."

"I just want to write words. Like I used to do on a typewriter."

"Typewriter?" He frowned at the unfamiliar term. "Maybe you'd be better just sticking with a Mac."

Which, for the sake of retaining my sanity, is what I ended up doing. The little G4 iBook I ordered trails behind some of its PC counterparts in both size and snuss, but when it arrives, all I'll have to do is install the Word For Mac software I already have and I'll be up and running.

With luck, Microsoft won't revamp the software for at least a couple of years, so until then I'll be able to enjoy the sense of security and familiarity my old Smith-Corona typewriter used to provide, and I'll be able to write letters and Cracker Barrel columns and maybe a novel or two without the uneasy sense that I'm working on borrowed time, a dull-witted dinosaur lumbering toward oblivion.

And who knows? Maybe by then the printed word itself will be regarded as obsolete, there'll be no need to replace my antiquated laptop, and I'll be spared the nerve-tingling adventure of picking and choosing from the wondrous buffet of modern gadgetry.

Lunch with the Prince

A week ago Monday my wife and I were feeling downcast. For the past eleven days we'd been exulting in the beauty of the Pacific Northwest, inhaling the sweet scent of cherry blossoms, delighting in the profusion of daffodils and crocuses, resting our snow-weary eyes on pleasurable swaths of rich green grass. And now it was time to leave.

Our friends in Vancouver, Bill and Jackie Walker (themselves Minnesotans who'd rented an apartment for the month of March and invited us out to visit), suggested we take one final swing through Stanley Park, the magnificent thousand-acre jewel at the north end of the city. "Let's drive along the seawall and look at all the sailboats and have lunch at The Teahouse."

We readily agreed. City parks are always fun to visit. But Stanley Park can have no equal. Thanks to the vision of Vancouver's founding fathers, this magnificent parcel of land has graced the city for over a hundred years, providing citizens and wildlife a sanctuary of breathtaking beauty and breath-giving oxygen. Laced with trails on which to walk or bike or skateboard and buffered on its seaward edge by several miles of stone seawall, the park boasts thousands of giant cedars and Douglas firs and uncountable shrubs and vines; a world-class Shangri-la available to everyone.

Driving along the seawall we passed a place called Prospect Point and noticed a parked contingent of shiny black Toyota limos along with a TV crew setting up for an interview. Some local bigwig, we surmised, and kept driving. When we came to the restaurant, we parked and went inside.

"Do you have reservations?" asked the waitress. Strange, we thought, this being a weekday morning.

"No."

"I'll see what I can do."

She returned a few minutes later, smiling, and escorted us into the glass-roofed wing of the building and gave us a place next to the window, overlooking the sea. We couldn't have asked for a more pleasant spot.

Then, shortly after we'd ordered, the contingent of limos pulled up outside, discharging a phalanx of bodyguards with stern faces and suspiciously bulging suit coats. They formed a protective wall around a dapper-looking chap and ushered him inside.

"Who's that?" we asked our waiter.

"Naruhito, the Crown Prince of Japan."

A moment later he entered the room, smiling and very much at ease. He walked past our table and was given a seat two tables away, together with several companions. He must have told a joke, for a moment later all of them were laughing.

"It's not every day you sit in the same room with royalty," said my wife.

"He sure doesn't seem stuck up," I noted, watching as he raised a glass in toast.

"The people of Japan like him," said Bill. "He's done a lot of charity work."

"I can't believe he's sitting there, a few feet away," said Jackie. "You'd think he'd be surrounded by secret service guys." There were, in fact, a couple of bodyguards positioned at a table at right angles to ours. But they, like us, were busy enjoying lunch. We lingered over dessert, fascinated by the matter-of-fact way the prince conducted himself, sharing in conversation with his companions but never seeming to dominate it. He sipped his wine, buttered his bread, and smiled in delight when the waiter served the main course, a salmon fillet cooked on a cedar plank.

Finally it was over and we made our way outside, still marveling at the serendipitous turn of events that had graced our last day in the city. We walked to the seawall and took one final look at the gulls and the sailboats and the ocean-going freighters and then turned to watch the limos pull into line and whisk the crown prince off to the airport for his return trip to Japan.

We, too, would soon be airborne, flying east while he went west. The only difference between us was that we'd be crammed in coach-class seats while he'd sprawl out in his own private jet.

But what the heck. At least we'd enjoyed a bit of lunch together.

Cornucopia

Wednesday night. Home from a hard day of work; sweaty, beat, and hungry.

"What's for supper?"

"You'll see," says my wife, a hint of mystery in her voice.

Hmmm. I hurry through a shower, grab a cold beer from the fridge, and head to the screen porch. Visions of sirloin dance through my head, but I haven't been asked to start the grill. Maybe pork chops, cooked inside? I sip the beer, scratch the cat's neck, close my eyes. Whatever it is, it'll be good. Fortunately, two benevolent events happened years ago: I was born in the USA and I married an excellent cook.

A few minutes later she calls out to say it's time to eat. I walk inside, help carry a few things to the table, sit down. The space between us is covered with bowls of various vegetables, arranged around a central dish of wild-rice brats and cherry tomatoes on angel-hair pasta coated with pesto that friends brought back from Italy. I light our memorial candle, put my napkin on my lap, and dig in.

Bowl after bowl yields mouthwatering treasure. Fresh green beans. Fresh broccoli. Tomatoes dripping seeds and juice. Sliced cucumbers floating in vinegar. I even try a helping of my wife's newest culinary love, Swiss chard, and find it rather tasty.

Later we sit outside in the lowering light and tell ourselves how incredibly lucky we are. Whether you grow your own garden, trade with a neighbor, visit a farmer's market, or frequent the produce section of your local store, late-summer food is abundant and delicious.

From here on till freeze-up, we're living in tall clover. Sweet corn, fresh potatoes, beets, radishes, onions, Brussels sprouts, rutabagas, peppers, zucchini: the list makes you dizzy with anticipation.

Thursday night we dined on BLT's, the lettuce crisp, the bacon crunchy, the tomatoes indescribable. For dessert we had fresh watermelon.

Friday night my wife cooked chicken breasts, a delectable bowl of mashed yellow potatoes, and a mélange of green beans, onions, sweet red peppers, mushrooms and zucchini all sautéed together.

How much better can life get? We are, after all, animals—and the first priority of all animals is to eat. We live in a country famed for its low food costs (roughly 15% of the average citizen's budget) and, while there are needy folk who deserve help in keeping their families healthy, the majority of us have plenty.

Now, as the days grow shorter and the first few yellow leaves appear, we rejoice in our good fortune and abundance, and revel in the cornucopia nature sets before us.

Taking Time

The summer our daughter was ten, I decided to take her out to lunch.

Just us. Dad and Kia. Nobody else.

I let her pick the place. She chose the Marina Restaurant at Breezy Point. She also planned out what she would wear, how to fix her hair, whether or not she should carry a purse.

When the appointed day came, I found myself assailed with second thoughts. I'd be missing half a day of work and spending money on something that suddenly seemed frivolous. Back then money was something we had little of, and time was something you didn't want to waste.

But when I offered her my arm and walked her to the car, all doubts vanished. She was radiant, proud, excited. In an instant, so was I.

At the restaurant we got a table overlooking the lake and ordered an appetizer to go with our non-alcoholic cocktails. We talked about gulls and water-skiers and how the summer sunlight danced on the water. I told her how beautiful she looked and how glad I was to be her dad. When the main course came we took our sweet time savoring it, and later we indulged ourselves with dessert.

Years afterward, she said it was one of her favorite memories, and I told her it was one of mine, too. In retrospect, it seemed magical. Just the two of us, all by ourselves, enjoying good food and a beautiful day and the chance to focus on one another without any distractions.

Looking back, I see that I enjoyed several such times, both with Kia and with our son, Chris, and also with my wife. But I also see that they were not very frequent, and that, if I could do it over, I'd try to arrange more of them.

It doesn't take much, you know. A few hours set aside for fishing. Maybe a Saturday afternoon walk in the autumn woods. An hour of moonlit swimming. An impromptu visit to an ice cream store. Whatever. The main thing is that you take the humdrum out of the commonplace, and make it into something unusual.

Years later, when Kia succumbed to cancer and was taken from us, the memory of that special day took on immeasurable importance. Now it stands as one of the happiest and most valuable memories of my entire life.

Next time you're tempted to take time for something out of the ordinary with someone you love, do it.

It's worth it. Worth every penny, every effort, every minute. It's what adds the sparkle and the grace notes to our otherwise habit-driven lives, and builds a treasure chest of golden memories.

Narrative

L ooking back over the many events and adventures of my life, I can't help but consider myself fortunate. I was blessed with intelligent and loving parents, surrounded by grandparents and aunts and uncles who taught and encouraged me, and I came in time to have four brothers and sisters and a beautiful wife, two splendid children who married equally splendid spouses, three marvelous grandkids, and many dear friends, all of whom have added ongoing sparkle and joy to my days. What more could a fellow ask?

Uncle Bill

My long-dead Uncle Bill must have been a lively kind of guy. Even now, some fifty-odd years after his passing, his spirit remains present in the family. Anecdotes about him persist, usually involving something done to excess. Which should come as no surprise, I suppose, since his lifelong motto consisted of these five words: *too much is just enough.*

The strange thing about Uncle Bill is that he was a very ordinary fellow. His big adventure in life was being a Navy man in World War I. After that he came home, settled down to a humdrum life as a mailman in Chicago and married Aunt Lill, family memories of whom are rather tart. She was apparently a whiner, always finding fault with something. Photos of her hint at little love of life. In an era when families tended toward large, they had no children. So Uncle Bill's life must have been rather constricted. Up before dawn, down to the post office, out on the streets with a heavy leather mailbag slung over his shoulder, day after week after year.

Yet the stories about him continue, and his famous motto lives on.

Why?

The only clue resides in my own very misty memories of the man. I can recall him hoisting me onto his lap, fixing me with his sparkling eyes, and launching into the story of Captain Ahab in search of the great white whale. I was barely past toddlerhood at the time, but the enthusiasm he brought to that story remains forever a part of me. Sitting there astride his knee, the regular world dimmed away and was replaced by foaming seas and plunging boats and razor-edged harpoons, the frenzy driven onward by the mad captain with the wooden leg.

Had Uncle Bill read *Moby Dick*? I don't know. Did he tell the story accurately? I don't know that, either. But I do know that he rendered me spellbound as I sat there with him, weaving magic with the sound of his voice and the piercing intensity of his eyes. He lifted me out of the ordinary and into the universe of the imagination—and therein lay his magnetism and power.

What did it matter that his outward life was strapped into endless routine? What difference did it make that his wife was shrewish, his prospects unremarkable? He had himself, and his memories, and his imagination. That was enough to transform the world into a wonderful, exciting place, where great adventures happened every day, and too much was just enough.

Uncle Henry

J ust before I fell asleep the other night, I thought about my
Uncle Henry. I hadn't thought about him for several years,
and the train of memories associated with his name moved
me to tears of remembered joy.

I must have been four or five when Uncle Henry decided to
take his week of vacation out in the country at my grandpa's cottage
in the little town of Long Lake, Illinois, some fifty miles north of
Chicago, where I was spending the summer.

We soon fell into a routine which, much to a small boy's delight,
we repeated every day. It started at the breakfast table.

Uncle Henry would pour a generous shot of milk into a final cup
of coffee, stir it slowly, and say, "Well, what do you think? Should
we hike up to the station and watch the train come in again?"

"You bet!"

His gentle eyes would sparkle at my obvious excitement. But
then he'd take a long sip of coffee and his face would darken with
seeming concern. "You think we dare take the shortcut?"

At that my heart would beat faster, thrilled and a little bit
terrified at the prospect of leaving the safety of the paved road in
favor of the winding path that led through a rock-strewn meadow

on the way toward town. He'd told me some of the scratch marks on the rocks might be Indian writing, and that walking cross-country could expose us to possible ambush. He never specified by whom, but the word "ambush" turned the prospect into high adventure.

"We better go single file," I'd say, pleased to repeat the new term he'd taught me.

"I agree."

A few minutes later we'd be on our way, walking hand-in-hand beneath the arching elm branches that towered above the streets of the little town. When we came to the place where the path through the meadow started, he'd whisper, "You go first. But be careful!" Pulse pounding, I'd lead the way, my eyes darting back and forth on high alert, nerve endings aquiver. When at length we reached the next road, we'd both let out loud sighs of relief, thankful to have made it across the dangerous shortcut without incident.

Later, at the railroad station, we'd sit on the wooden bench eating pieces of saltwater taffy Uncle Henry had bought across the street at Nix's Grocery. They must have been his favorite, because he bought them every day. We'd take our time carefully unwrapping each piece and, in-between chews, we'd talk about the weather and the shapes of the clouds and how nice the earth smelled after a good rain.

Then Uncle Henry would pull out his pocket watch and say, "Any minute now," and we'd swivel around on the bench in hopes of catching sight of the incoming train. Back then train engines were something to behold: huge, black, steam-and-smoke-belching monsters with drive wheels as tall as a grown man, the wheels linked together with coupling rods which, as they swiveled up and down and back and forth, were almost guaranteed to hypnotize you.

"Thar she blows!" I'd sing out, using the phrase my Uncle Bill, a Navy man, had taught me. We'd stand up, eyes riveted on the approaching black locomotive spewing a cloud of white smoke. On it would come, its rumble audible now, the earth beginning to vibrate under its enormous weight. As it grew closer, Uncle Henry would put his hand on my shoulder and say, "I don't see any cows on the cowcatcher," and I'd nod, relieved, sure that one day our luck would run out and there'd be a mangled farm animal draped over the lattice of steel bars that angled down in front of the engine.

We'd stand at respectful attention as the train slowed to a stop, watch as the conductor swung down from the passenger car to place his steel step on the platform, wait till the handful of travelers disembarked and another handful climbed aboard. Then we'd wave to the engineer and watch the drive wheels start to turn, and sometimes they'd break traction and suddenly spin, and the coupling rods would move in a blur as the slow rhythmic *chuff chuff chuff* of the escaping steam compressed itself into an angry hiss.

We'd watch until the end of the train disappeared around a long curve. Then Uncle Henry would take my hand in his and we'd start the walk home. This time there'd be no talk of shortcuts, for which I was secretly thankful.

Looking back, I realize Uncle Henry understood the importance of moderation. After all, a person can handle only so much excitement in a single morning. And we'd already limited out.

Ongoing Promise

Living here in the great north woods confers both benefits and challenges.

In exchange for the gifts of pristine air and the ancient tremolo of loons, we forsake ready access to the Mall of America and the Metrodome. In place of the treasures contained in the Minneapolis Art Institute, we focus on sunsets and rainbows. Denied the nearby thrill of skyscrapers and Guthrie plays, we take delight in tall pines and the drama of unfolding seasons.

Summer here brings many pleasures. One of the greatest is the chance to witness things coming of age. During this magical respite from winter, an important lesson grows clear: the beat of life goes on.

Two weeks ago I glanced out the window at the suet feeder and saw what looked like two woodpeckers kissing. A closer look revealed the truth: a male downy feeding his clueless young. He'd peck off a chunk of suet, turn toward a waiting youth, and push it gently into the opened beak. Two young ones vied for Dad's attention; Dad, in turn, took turns. First a chunk for one, then one for the other. By the end of the day the kids were taking tentative stabs at the suet themselves, no longer waiting for Father.

The following day the domestic drama was repeated, this time by two larger hairies. Same tree, same suet, different birds.

Two days after that, while I was driving out to get the mail, a mother grouse and her five chicks tried to cross the unpaved road ahead of me. I stopped, cut the engine, and watched. The chicks, mere puffballs of tannish fuzz, tried hard to follow Mom across the driveway. Two inches long, their stubby wings still featherless, they wobbled uncertainly over the irregular terrain. One tried to change course and toppled over, shook its head, and struggled upright. Several minutes later, the little line of fledglings finally reached the other side and disappeared into the tall grass.

Later that day, returning from town, I was treated to the sight of a white-tailed doe and two speckled fawns. And a few nights later, sitting watching a Twins game on TV, my wife and I became aware of five dark shapes moving across the terrace toward the bird feeder. When we flicked on the outdoor light, we were greeted by an adult raccoon and four youngsters foraging for supper.

Since spring, we've seen two clutches of fledgling phoebes burst into their first flight. We've watched young robins splashing in the birdbath. We've followed the antics of newborn cottontails, seen little red squirrels play tag in our oak trees, and watched lines of infant mallards and wood ducks swim along behind their parents. This time of year brings with it the profound promise of ongoing life. The sight of so many young creatures launching off on the great adventure of living brings a fullness to those of us farther down the path.

Life goes on. The circle is unbroken.

Fresh Start

It's the Fourth of July, 2007. Our house bustles with family and friends as they joke and jostle about, glad to be together. The weather's ideal, a classic summer day, perfect for celebrating our country's birth as a sovereign nation.

"Here," says my daughter-in-law, Sara, handing me our latest grandchild, not quite two months old. "Try to get him to burp."

I hold young Jack, pull the side of the swaddling blanket away from his face. His eyes stare up toward mine as if to ask, "Who are you?"

"I'm your grandpa," I murmur, smiling.

His eyes move down to my beard. "What's that?" he seems to ask. "Why do you have hair on the bottom of your face?"

"Just for the fun of it," I explain. "Maybe someday I'll shave it off. Maybe someday you'll decide to grow one." I try to imagine a two-month-old sporting whiskers. "Or maybe not."

He opens his mouth as if to speak, then closes it and sighs. I touch his lower lip with my finger and wonder: Will this young fellow always have plenty to eat? The world is changing; our species now numbers more than six billion, heading toward seven. The competition for food can't help but intensify as the century moves along. And what of other resources such as oil and timber and water and land? Will the supply prove adequate to the demand?

Jack yawns. I smile again. "That's right. No worries, little guy. You'll do just fine." But inwardly I wonder. We Americans are used to wallowing in plenty. It's been three or four generations since the Great Depression. Granted, for the past several years we've been telling ourselves that we've got to change our ways, that our current habits of consumption are simply not sustainable. But will we change in time to avert widespread shortages? I hope so.

I cradle my grandson up against my shoulder and pat him on the back. "Burping's good," I whisper. "Go ahead and get the air out."

He wiggles his head from side to side and I feel the softness of his cheek against my face. What a marvelous little bundle this young fellow is! Tiny, fragile, and utterly dependent—yet capable of growing into a strong, resilient adult.

Inside this little body lies enormous strength of purpose. Within a scant few years he'll learn to walk and talk and reason, find a way to make his needs and desires known, take his rightful place among the teeming herd known as humanity. For all I know, he might become the next Bill Gates or Brett Favre or Brad Pitt. Or better yet, Joe Mauer.

"My turn," says my wife, holding out her arms to take him. Young Jack is in demand. He's already been held by half a dozen people, and he's only been here half an hour.

"Umm," says Claire, lifting him to her face. "You smell good." I watch as she strokes his hair and tells him how handsome he is. I feel the worries about tomorrow evaporate like the morning dew.

Whatever Jack's future, one thing is clear. Like his brother, Levi, and his sister, Grace, this little boy is well loved.

A Long Walk

E ver wonder where you came from?

"Sure," you say, "and I know. Great-grandpa Lars came from Norway and married great-grandma Hilda, who emigrated from Austria."

But what happened before that? I mean, way back; not just a hundred years or two, but thousands.

"Impossible," you say. "That's ancient history. You can't go back that far."

Ah, but you can. Thanks to a recent genetic history project, it's now possible to trace the roots of your family tree back many thousands of years. The project, titled "Genographic," is a five-year research partnership between National Geographic and IBM, funded by the Waitt Family Foundation, and involves participants from all around the world.

The key to unlocking the mysteries of the past is DNA (deoxyribonucleic acid), a molecule that's the major component of chromosomes and which carries genetic information, resulting in traits that range from eye color and height to athleticism and disease susceptibility. Each of us carries a combination of genes passed from both our mother and our father. One exception is the Y chromosome, which is passed directly from father to son, unchanged, from generation to generation.

But every so often a mutation—a random, naturally occurring, usually harmless change—occurs. When that happens, the mutation, known as a marker, acts as a beacon, and can be mapped through generations, because it will be passed down from the man in whom it occurred to his sons, their sons, and every male in the family for thousands of years. Each marker is essentially the beginning of a new lineage on the family tree of the human race. Tracking the lineages provides a picture of how small tribes of humans diversified thousands of years ago and spread to populate the world.

Participants in the Genographic project provide researchers with two samples of genetic material. Results of the analysis are recorded and a printout returned to you via computer. Since the project is in its infancy, the results provided are generalized and somewhat sketchy, but nonetheless fascinating.

In my own case, it appears my forebears emerged out of Africa (where apparently all human life began) roughly 50,000 years ago and migrated north across the Arab peninsula, probably in reaction to a climate change brought on by the melting of northern European ice sheets.

Some ten thousand years later, as indicated by a second genetic marker known as M9, they turned east and migrated into present-day Tajikistan. Later the group split in two, with some heading south into Pakistan and India, while others, including my forebears, moved north into Central Asia.

The next genetic marker, M45, indicates a clan that gave rise to the common ancestors of most Europeans and nearly all Native Americans.

Reacting to the hostile conditions of a new Ice Age, they again split apart, with some heading east toward the Pacific (and, eventually, North America) and the others moving west toward Europe.

Further markers show the movement of my forebears onto the European subcontinent, eventually becoming part of the dominant group known as Cro-Magnon—the peoples responsible for the famous cave paintings found in southern France. These ancestors knew how to make woven clothing using the natural fibers of plants, and had relatively advanced tools of stone, bone, and ivory. Over time they spread throughout Europe, and many generations later gave rise to both my maternal and paternal great-grandfathers, who lived on the shore of the Baltic Sea in northern Germany.

The research results include a map showing the probable path my forebears took as they moved through fifty thousand years of time. Studying it, I couldn't help but marvel. It was a very long walk.

Impressions of Japan

"East is East and West is West, and never the twain shall meet," wrote Rudyard Kipling.

But that was before the advent of nonstop flights from Minneapolis to Tokyo. Now it's common as rain for travelers to eat breakfast here in Minnesota and enjoy supper in Japan. While the change in time zones (15 hours difference) means supper is half a day late, the flight itself lasts a mere twelve hours.

Thus it was that my wife and I recently spent two glorious weeks in the land of the rising sun, visiting her brother, Ron, and his Japanese wife, Sumiko. They'd been inviting us to come for years, and since they both speak fluent English as well as Japanese, and none of us is getting any younger, we figured it was time to go.

On the way over, I confess I nurtured certain worries about food. Tales of visitors gagging on squid and whale blubber did little to calm my stomach. But such fears were misplaced. From start to end, the meals we ate were downright delicious. And while I did find squid unpleasantly chewy and whale blubber inedible, such fare was more than offset by the cornucopia of mouthwatering vegetables and fruit and fish and chicken and rice that we enjoyed throughout the trip.

Many of our meals, especially at suppertime, were a succession of dishes placed in the middle of the table and shared by all. We found this delightful. You take a bit of everything, lifting it carefully with your chopsticks to your own little plate and from there to your mouth. It makes you eat slowly, and allows you to savor the taste of each item, all the while talking and laughing and enjoying the company of your tablemates.

Another pleasant surprise was the nationwide presence of vending machines filled with piping hot tins of coffee, cocoa, and soup (their warmth identified by red buttons) and cold pop and fruit juice and beer (their coolness signified by blue.) Wherever you went, refreshment was nearby.

Then there was the joy of traveling on trains. Japan is laced with trains, most of them powered electrically, and whether slow-moving commuter lines or 160 mile-per-hour bullet trains, all of them run punctually. The cars are clean, the seats comfortable, the ambience generally relaxed (though the commuter trains get crowded at rush hour). It's a pleasure to travel this way, unworried about traffic jams or weather conditions.

Everywhere we went, we were struck by how well things worked, and how courteous the people were. According to Ron, Japan is blessedly free of such things as road rage, gang wars, and slums. There is some theft and occasional acts of violence, but the incidence of such things is a fraction of what occurs here in America. We felt as safe in the streets of downtown Tokyo at midnight as we would in Minneapolis at noon, and every time we encountered someone at an elevator, a doorway, or intersection, they motioned for us to go ahead of them.

There is, in short, an air of civility and good manners in Japan that we found refreshing. And the Japanese have not hesitated to build some of these values into their infrastructure. In Tokyo we noticed yellow tiles embedded in many of the sidewalks, some of them cast in the form of parallel bars, others with a grid of dots. Sumiko explained that these allowed blind folks to find their way by feeling the bars and dots beneath their feet, the bars indicating straight ahead, the dots an intersection. Installing such sidewalk Braille systems must have cost billions and billions of yen. But there they are, a tangible testament to Japanese values, along with universal health care and an effective educational system which includes a wide range of vocational training programs for those students not going to college.

One aspect of Japan that turned us off was the sheer number of people. With a population a bit less than half ours (128 million) crowded into a country the size of Montana, space is at a premium. Since the land itself is predominantly mountainous, the actual habitable area is roughly 20 percent of the total, so you end up with all those millions living cheek by jowl. As a result, land costs are exorbitant, houses are generally small, roads are narrow, and cars and trucks downsized. The good news, of course, is that living on such a scale results in significant energy savings, and that's something the Japanese have taken seriously. Everywhere we went we saw clothing hung outside to dry, thus saving the use of a clothes dryer, and countless buildings sported rooftops clad with heat collectors and solar-voltaic panels.

While we didn't drive much in Japan, we were impressed with how skillfully other drivers negotiated narrow clearances and crowded streets. Ron told us the legal driving age there is 20, which is also the age at which one can officially vote and drink. Most cars, busses, bikes and even work trucks were carefully washed and polished, and we noticed an amazing lack of litter anywhere. Since smoking is limited to designated areas in cities, there are no cigarette butts on the ground. The taxicabs we took were spotless, their drivers smartly dressed and wearing white gloves.

I could go on and on, and mention items such as heated toilet seats and a nationwide courier service that can move your luggage from city to city and the joy of staying at traditional country inns with tatami mats and futons and sliding soshi screens, and the leg-cramping agony of eating at tables eight inches off the floor. But better, I think, to leave such discoveries to you, the reader.

Whether you see it in person or enjoy it via printed page or travel channel, Japan is a magical place, and one well worth your time.

Narrative

For those of us nearing the end of life, the future at times seems anything but encouraging. Compared to the beckoning adventures that greeted us in youth, circumstances now appear daunting. A global population of seven billion and rising; the clouds of carbon dioxide and other pollution that rise along with it; increasing worries about food and energy production and our seeming inability to find ways of living in sustainable balance with our lovely planet; these and other concerns push many thoughtful citizens toward despair.

But uncertain as the future may appear, it is the place toward which life invariably moves, and as such merits our acceptant blessing. Our children and our children's children will live in the house of tomorrow, not yesterday. Their loyalty belongs to that which is yet to come. To harp instead upon the imagined superiority of that which has already passed is ultimately pointless. It discourages where hope is most needed, and does none of us any good.

The world abounds with countless wonders, each of which invites respect and celebration. As members of the species blessed with unremitting consciousness, it's our job to notice goodness and competence and beauty, and to share that awareness in every way we can.

A Perfect Day

S aturday, July 25, 2009. I wake to the call of a loon. It's a little past seven. If this were a workday, it would be late. But today it's just right. We're renting a cabin on East Twin Lake, and we're on vacation.

I shuffle into the bathroom, splash water on my face, brush my teeth, grin at the mirror. Today's the final day of what's proved to be a wonderful week. We've spent it with our grandkids, Levi, 9, and Grace, 7, with occasional visits from two-year-old Jack. We've had lots of adventures, fishing and swimming, canoeing, picking raspberries, playing Boggle, watching Hannah Montana on TV, rooting for Levi's baseball team in its final game of the season, watching Grace practice doing cartwheels, collecting snail shells, sailing in the rain. Now it's nearly over.

The seductive smell of fresh coffee lures me to the kitchen and from there out to the deck, where my wife sits working a crossword puzzle. "Sleep well?" I ask. "You bet," she says. "What about you?" "Like a rock." Our little exchange hides a larger truth: taking care of youngsters uses up a surprising amount of energy. But the past several days have been fun, and a glance out at the lake promises more to come. The surface is dappled with waves, which means there's wind, which means we can take the sailboat out for a final run.

A few hours later we're ready to go. Grace has decided to stay ashore with Grandma. Levi starts the little outboard while I raise the jib and check the mainsail. We putter away from the dock. I tidy up a few tangled ropes and lower the centerboard all the way down. Levi's young hand is steady on the tiller. We motor out into the bay. "OK?" he asks. "Perfect." He kills the engine as the wind fills the sails and tilts us to port. In the sudden silence we look at each other and smile. "I love it when it's just the wind," he says.

We settle into a steady reach, aimed toward the opposite shore. Water burbles beneath the hull. The wind hums in the rigging. We pass within twenty feet of a lone loon, who watches us go by without concern. A seagull swoops down as if to inspect us, then glides away in a long curving arc.

Our little boat is nothing fancy. Fifteen feet long, it sports two modest sails and a small cabin. Earlier in the week, Grace and her cousin, Kassie, sat in the sailboat's cabin eating peanut butter sandwiches while my wife and I sailed along in the rain. Because the cabin is little, kids seem to love it. But it's not very comfortable for adults.

We near the south shore of the lake and come about. I'm pleased to see that Levi knows just what to do. We switch sides in the cockpit, readjust the sails, and start back down the lake. The sun warms our skin and sends sparkles of skittering light against our faces. The hum of the wind and the murmur of the water lull us into quiet reverie.

We're here, now, sailing along in the middle of a beautiful little lake, glad to be alive and glad to be together. What more could a person want?

Remembering

For much of the year just past, I've been working on writing a memoir about boyhood. The work has not proceeded smoothly, but rather by fits and starts. A scene here, a character there, now and then a recollected incident, followed by a week or two of maddening blankness.

Most of the summer passed with little progress. For several weeks I walked around second-guessing my efforts. Maybe the whole idea was foolish. Maybe I'd waited too long before starting; whole chunks of childhood seem to have melted away, like arctic ice floes in an ever-warming world.

Then came a letter from a friend in England, herself a writer with several published novels to her credit, telling me about an interesting insight regarding memory. Seems some recent experiments about consciousness and perception uncovered a strange but significant fact.

"Apparently," wrote my friend, "just *writing* the words 'I remember' is a way of bringing up memories. It's not enough to *say* it, or to type it, but with pen on paper, it's reputed to be infallible. I thought about your current book and wondered if this would be worth trying if you get stuck."

Skeptical—but willing to try most anything—I gave it a whirl. At first it merely felt peculiar. I'm used to composing sentences on the computer keyboard, not on a sheet of paper. Over the years, from lack of use, my penmanship's grown almost illegible. But a strange thing happened.

When I wrote down "I remember," my pen seemed to want to keep going of its own accord: "I remember the time we were fishing at the Broken Down Bridge and all of a sudden we heard a loud *whump* and the water in the channel rose up a fraction and then subsided, leaving wet marks on all the wooden pilings."

I stared at the sentence in disbelief. Where, I wondered, did that particular memory come from? Other details came crowding back. How my buddy, Bruce Nelson, and I had left our fishing poles on the ground and gone running toward where we thought the sound had come from; how it turned out that an excavator had ruptured a natural-gas line, which caused the explosion that started the Wagners' house on fire; how, luckily, there was no one inside; how the house burned with an unbelievable intensity, scorching the siding and roof shingles of its neighbors thirty feet away in spite of the fact that the firemen had their hoses trained on the adjoining buildings much of the time.

A few days later I tried the experiment again. "I remember . . . playing tennis with a girl named Nancy Hocking at the campground in Upper Michigan by Fortune Lake. We were both maybe eleven or twelve and she had reddish brown hair and freckles and wore braces on her teeth. Later I found out she had leukemia and died that winter."

This time I stared at the sentence through a swirl of unbidden tears. I hadn't thought about Nancy for dozens of years. The remembrance of her dying at such a young age was still outrageous.

I have no explanation for what took place. I can't explain why an excavator happened to hit a gas line and blow up Wagners' house. I can't explain why a sweetie like Nancy Hocking should have died before reaching teenhood. And I can't explain why writing the words "I remember" should happen to trigger such memories.

But I do know that all these things happened.

Axe Man

Y ou, dear reader, probably don't believe that at my advanced age I actually bought a brand-new electric bass guitar, and am fitfully learning to play it. But it's true.

A bit of background may help explain this seemingly rash act. Many decades ago, when the world was younger and more innocent and I still lived near Chicago, I learned to play the bass viol, the big old stand-up bass, like a cello on steroids, that was a fixture in every rock and jazz combo in the nation. I played the bass for a couple of years and, in the process, had a lot of fun and made some extra money. Then, abruptly, I grew up and moved to Minnesota, and that was the end of that. It was time to put away youthful follies and start acting like an adult. Get serious. Get a job. Get a wife. Settle down.

So I did. I became a no-nonsense wage earner, placing my nose against the grindstone and keeping it there for decades, just like everybody else. No time for tomfoolery, for wasting time in the grasshoppery pursuit of musical pleasure. No sir, not me. I was serious. I was grown up. And I was tuneless.

Then, a couple of years ago, I got to wondering if I hadn't made a horrible mistake. As a young man, music had been a regular part of my life, a steady source of joy. Maybe I'd overreacted by turning my back on it. Why not buy a bass and resume playing? But not a big old stand-up bass. Better to get something smaller and easier to move around.

Why not, indeed? Aside from the obvious fact that my fingers are a bit gnarly from decades of work as a stonemason, and the even more obvious fact that I don't seem to learn new things as rapidly as I used to, why not?

Thus it was that in early December I took delivery of a brand-new Squire Fender electric jazz bass, together with a 15-watt practice amp, a digital tuner, and a digital metronome. The instrument (or axe, as we wild-haired musicians like to call it) is a thing of surpassing beauty, with a black body, white strike plate, maple neck, and rosewood fret board. The neck is slim and elegant, and fits my hand just right. Each time I slip the strap over my neck, plug in the cord, and flick the amplifier on, a little tremor of joy vibrates through my bones.

I don't want to minimize the difficulty I'm having learning to play a new instrument. The electric bass and the stand-up viol are two very different things. Local axe men need not worry that I'll ever be challenging them for a gig. If I learn to play "Twinkle, Twinkle Little Star" before they cart me off to the rest home, I'll probably be doing well.

But none of that bothers me at all. Every afternoon I'm back for another session, hunched over my wonderful instrument, intent on learning to make a joyful noise.

My only regret is that I didn't start doing it years ago.

Change of Plans

Punta Gorda, Florida, 2010. It's Friday and the special day is here. Today we're scheduled to drive south to Fort Myers to watch the Twins play the New York Mets. We bought the tickets months ago, and our excitement's been building ever since.

There's nothing like spring training. You get to stand right next to the players, say hello to some of them, maybe even get some autographs. Our grandkids are excited, too. Levi, our oldest, now ten, practically worships Joe Mauer. Grace, just turned eight, is looking forward to her first major-league game. And Jack, not quite three, is automatically up for everything.

Then the rain begins. With it comes the wind.

I sit in the lanai sipping coffee and try to think positive thoughts. "We'll be okay if it stops by ten," I say to my wife. "The game doesn't start till one o'clock, and the field'll be dry by then."

By ten the shower has escalated to a downpour. Wind whistles through the palm tree outside the lanai, whipping the fronds to a mad green frenzy. I squint toward the west and see nothing but gray. Our son, Chris, and his wife, Sara, arrive from their motel with the grandkids, rain dripping from their baseball caps. I get on the phone and confirm the bad news. The game's been cancelled, and during

208

spring training there are no make-up games. We're just plain out of luck.

What to do? "We could try to see some manatees," I suggest. There's a county park on a river north of Fort Myers where the discharged water from a power plant raises the temperature of the stream and the manatees sometimes come to get warm. "If the rain lets up, it might be fun."

The crestfallen faces of the kids brighten. A manatee hunt! Why not? Sara elects to stay behind and wash clothes. The rest of us pile in the car and head south. On the way, the rain lessens. Things are looking up. But twenty minutes later, as we drive into the park, a renewed torrent of water hits the windshield. "Did we remember to bring the . . . ?" No. The umbrellas are back at the condo.

We sit in the car, hoping the rain will slacken. The windows fog up and the troops grow restless. "Tell you what," I say. "I'll run down to the river and see what's happening." I jerk the door open and hurry across the parking lot. In less than a minute I'm sopped to the skin. But when I get to the river, a manatee comes to the surface a dozen yards away. I turn and hurry back to the car, and moments later we're all splashing through the downpour to view the strange creatures.

"Look!" yells Levi, pointing toward a surfacing behemoth. "It's gotta weigh a ton!" He may be right, since the largest of these water mammals can tip the scales at over 3000 pounds, though most weigh far less. We stare through the slicing rain in wonder, amazed that such a giant can move with such grace.

We huddle under the partial shelter of a tin-roofed viewing platform as the wind rises to gale force and the pelting rain sizzles on the surface of the river. We're absolutely drenched, but nobody seems to care. The kids grin as rainwater drips from their chins and oozes through their tennis shoes.

Here, in the presence of these gentle giants, our hearts are glad.

A Magical Place

As regular readers of the Cracker Barrel know, I spent most of my working life as a stonemason. Given this fact, you can imagine the excitement I felt last week when, together with my wife and the friends we were traveling with, I had the chance to visit a stone castle in the making.

The castle's located in France, some ninety miles south of Paris, in the province of Burgundy, and takes its name from the woods in which it stands: Chateau de Guédelon.

A historian's dream, Guédelon is being built by some 35 enthusiasts using only the tools, techniques, and materials available in the 13th century, and is based on drawings drafted in 1228. Characterized by their quadrangular ground plans and cylindrical towers, royal castles such as the Louvre in Paris and Dourdan in Essonne served as models for feudal lords in the construction of their own strongholds. Guédelon is part of that tradition.

When complete, it will include four towers surrounding a central courtyard with a bridge and a moat, as well as a large living space. The goal of the project is to give visitors a better appreciation of medieval construction and for the builders to learn about medieval techniques while they work.

Ground was broken in 1997, on the site of an abandoned stone quarry, but the castle won't be finished until 2025 or later. The height of its walls currently varies from ten to twenty-five feet tall, with the tallest parts being the Great Tower, twelve meters in diameter and projected to reach a height of 28.5 meters, and the Great Hall, enclosed within the protective outer walls and containing huge storerooms, garderobes (toilets), a kitchen, a meeting hall, and the imaginary lord's bedchamber.

Visitors enter the project to the sound of chisels chipping rock and the sight of workers dressed in medieval garb. Everything involved in building Guédelon is produced right on the site. Sandstone building blocks are quarried from the earth, as is clay for the floor and roof tiles, and sand for the making of mortar. Small thatched-roof huts house the workshops of a weaver, who spins and dyes her own yarn; a ropemaker who regales onlookers with his chatter of caustic humor; and a basket maker responsible for producing several dozen baskets per month, which are used to haul mortar and small stone and tend to wear out rather quickly.

Other open-sided buildings protect the teams of carpenters and blacksmiths so vital to the project. The carpenters cut oaks in the surrounding forest and fashion tool handles, carts, cart wheels, hoisting mechanisms, roof beams, scaffolding, shingles, and dozens of other objects from the wood. The blacksmiths make all the chisels, nails, hinges, straps, hammer heads, door handles, and other metal items in their wood-fired forge, as well as spending hours every day tempering and retempering the tools used to dress the stone.

Material is moved with horse-drawn carts. Bread is baked in the Great Hall ovens. The pace of work proceeds slowly, as befits a nonmechanized enterprise. The workers responsible for building Guédelon have come from all over France, and some from foreign lands. Their smiles and laughter speak volumes. The work is difficult and very physical. It's also clearly very satisfying.

To view the magic happening at Guédelon, visit the website at www.guedelon.fr.

Pages From the Past

S everal years ago my mom handed me a box of old letters. "From the war," she said, which for her meant WWII. "You might enjoy reading some of them."

I thanked her and put them on the shelf. Busy, busy, busy. Then, last month, two years after her death, I finally opened the box and plunged in.

Most of the letters are dated 1944, the year my dad, at age 33, got drafted into service. The bulk of them were sent to him at Camp Joseph T. Robinson, somewhere in Arkansas, where he was undergoing basic training.

The envelopes all carry three-cent stamps and sport no zip codes, since there weren't any then. A handful of postcards made the trip from Chicago to Arkansas at the postcard rate of one cent. And comments in the letters make it clear that, if you were in the service and writing to someone else on active duty, your mail went free of charge.

As might be expected, the letters contain no earthshaking news or lightning spears of insight. Most of them were evidently written at work during lunchtime, typed on the manual typewriters of the time, with four or five gals taking turns at the machines to dash letters off to their husbands or boyfriends. A few contain complaints about the faintness of the ribbons, with occasional apologies for typos. But in all of them the tone is positive, despite the fact that times were turbulent and the future anything but certain.

Like letters written today to a loved one stationed in Iraq or Afghanistan, most of the news was domestic in nature, with comments about Aunt Ella's health, the price of pork chops, difficulties with the oil furnace, plans to spend a weekend at Grandpa's cottage at the lake.

Given the fact that many consumer goods were rationed, there are constant references to thrift. "I'll have to cut down on gas if we expect to go anywhere if you come home on furlough in September," says one. "I've only got 15 gallons worth of coupons."

"The tire is just like new," says another, "now that Uncle Charlie had it vulcanized."

"Went to the early movie with (sister) Betty," she writes. "Saw Bing Crosby in 'Going My Way,'" The unspoken message is clear: the early show cost less than the regular evening one.

But the scrimping did not extend to thoughts of the future. Whether through furlough or leave or the eventual end of the war, she hearkened over and over to when they would be reunited, and made clear her readiness to celebrate. "Incidentally," she writes, "that ham sandwich and glass of beer will be waiting for you when you come, so hurry up as fast as you can."

This spirit of determination pervades the letters. No matter what, she insists on seeing the future as hopeful. But there are poignant moments when the economic as well as the emotional realities hit home. Dad, a buck private, was paid the munificent sum of $21 per month. At his behest, an allotment for his widowed mother, as well as one for Mom and my two-year-old self, were taken automatically from his pay, leaving him seven dollars a month with which to buy whatever the Army didn't supply. In letter after letter Mom makes mention of his plight and hopes he is somehow making do.

Finally she writes the following, which nearly 70 years later sums up the difference between yesterday and today: "Enclosed is $1. Thought you might make use of it until I get paid and can send more."

Acknowledgements

As mentioned in the preface to this book, I am forever indebted to Martha Anderson and her late husband, Keith, for originally inviting me to write an ongoing column in the Lake Country Echo, and for cheering on my early efforts. More recently, I owe recurring thanks to editor Nancy Vogt, publisher Pete Mohs, and the rest of the staff at Echo Publishing for producing a new edition of the paper every week and in the process creating a venue for my column, "The Cracker Barrel."

I also appreciate the hundreds of loyal readers who over the years have taken the time to express their appreciation of—or occasional disagreement with—some of the pieces I've written, and am deeply grateful to the many family members and friends whose constancy and moral support have proved unflagging.

Finally, I wish to thank the following individuals for their particular contributions: Tenlee Lund, for her professional editing skills and contagious encouragement; fellow writer and retired professor of history Art Lee, for the kind and generous endorsement he provided for the back cover of this book; veteran photographer and retired professor of biology John Hess, for the patience, skill, and enthusiasm he exhibited in producing the cover photo of the book; Crystal Tura, author's representative at AuthorHouse, for her relentless cheerfulness and knowledge while guiding me through the submission process; and, as always, my wife, Claire, for her computer skills, impeccable proofreading, vast and loving patience, and relentless intelligence and good sense.

Author Bio

Craig Nagel lives in the woods near Pequot Lakes, Minnesota, with his wife, Claire. He divides his time between writing, reading, traveling, sailing, taking naps, and having fun with his grandkids.